*Why Do I Need You
To Love Me In Order To
Like Myself*

# WHY DO I NEED YOU TO LOVE ME IN ORDER TO LIKE MYSELF

*How to Stop Your Need for Approval from Destroying Your Relationship and Your Life*

Barry Lubetkin, Ph.D. and
Elena Oumano, Ph.D.

While the case studies described in this book are based on interviews with real people, the names, professions, locations, and other biographical details about the participants have been changed to preserve their privacy and anonymity.

Section from *Thinking, Feeling, Behaving: An Emotional Education Curriculum for Adolescents* by A. Vernon, 1989 (Champaign, IL: Research Press). Copyright 1989 by the author. Reprinted by permission.

*Cover design by Frank Stinga*

Library of Congress Cataloging-in-Publication Data

Lubetkin, Barry.
    Why do I need you to love me in order to like myself : how to stop your need for approval from destroying your relationship and your life / by Barry Lubetkin and Elena Oumano. — 1st ed.
        p.    cm.
    ISBN 0-681-41457-X
    1. Rejection (Psychology)    2. Social acceptance.
3. Interpersonal relations.    4. Self-esteem—Social aspects—Problem, exercises, etc.    5. Cognitive therapy.
I. Oumano, Elena.    II. Title.
BF575.R35L83    1992
158—dc20                                    92-15335
                                            CIP

Printed in the United States

First Edition

0  9  8  7  6  5  4  3  2  1

# C O N T E N T S

INTRODUCTION

CHAPTER 1
APPROVAL-CRAVING:
THE SYNDROME AND ITS SYMPTOMS     /     27

CHAPTER 2
ASSESSING THE ORIGINS
OF YOUR APPROVAL CRAVING     /     57

CHAPTER 3
IDENTIFYING UNHEALTHY THOUGHTS
AND STYLES OF DISTORTED THINKING     /     77

CHAPTER 4
DO YOU CRAVE APPROVAL FROM EVERYONE?
TAKING STOCK OF YOUR APPROVAL-CRAVING
BEHAVIORS ON THE JOB, AND WITH STRANGERS,
THE FAMILY, AND FRIENDS     /     99

CHAPTER 5
DEVELOPING A PHILOSOPHY OF
SELF-ESTEEM THAT LASTS     /     117

CHAPTER 6
STOPPING DISAPPROVAL ANXIETY IN ITS
TRACKS THROUGH RELAXATION, DESENSITIZATION,
FLOODING, AND VISUALIZATION     /     127

CHAPTER 7

## RISK-TAKING AND SHAME ATTACK EXERCISES THAT WILL RID YOU OF SHAME AND EMBARRASSMENT ONCE AND FOR ALL / 142

CHAPTER 8

## HOW TO HELP YOUR CHILD OVERCOME HIS CRAVING FOR APPROVAL / 155

SUMMARY / 176

# INTRODUCTION

♦

## A Day in a Life

Tina's day begins when she awakens from a nightmare. After spilling a drink on her employer at an office party, Tina looks at her drenched boss and begins laughing uncontrollably. Humiliated, she is asked to leave. The alarm rescues Tina from her dream predicament, but she must silence the ringer immediately. If her husband wakes, she'll land in a real-life dilemma. Tina habitually rises a full hour and a half before Ernie so that she can have the bathroom to herself for a long, complicated toilet requiring an arsenal of beauty and hairstyling supplies.

Tina never allows Ernie to see her without her makeup and hairstyle intact. And she doesn't dare risk his anger in case he cannot use the bathroom when he wants. Furthermore, Ernie likes his breakfast ready as soon as he gets out of the bathroom. As Tina slips quietly out of bed, she tugs her nightgown down hastily just in case her husband awakes. If he should see those extra five pounds padding her waist, there'll be trouble. Ernie insists Tina maintain a perfect size six.

As Tina serves Ernie his bacon and pancakes, she reminds him of her sister's dinner party that evening. Tina is particularly eager to make a good appearance because her sister is considerably more well off. The sister has two groomed, well-behaved children, wears expensive clothes, drives a luxurious new car, and, unlike Tina, doesn't have to work. Tina shops the sales and Ernie says they can't afford children just now.

Tina climbs into her own ancient wreck and has trouble starting it. She remembers with irritation it was just last week that she paid three hundred dollars for repairs and still had trouble starting the car when she left the garage. The serviceman had airily attributed the problem to cold weather. As usual, Tina hadn't challenged his shaky explanation.

During the course of the workday, Tina overhears—for what seems like the thousandth time—her boss refer to her as his "girl." Tina is annoyed but says nothing. At a meeting on a department project, a colleague presents a proposal as entirely his own brain-child, although Tina contributed a substantial share of the ground-work. Tina hesitates to object for fear of offending the colleague whose position is somewhat higher than her own.

At lunch, her toast is burned, but Tina says nothing for fear of alienating the waitress at the coffee shop where she eats every day. After lunch, she presents the findings on research her boss asked her to do. Terrified, Tina manages to stammer her way through her presentation, then slinks back to her chair, convinced she made a fool of herself. At 4:30, her boss throws an hour's or more work on her desk as he strolls out the door. Tina wanted to get home in time to prepare for her sister's dinner party, but, as usual, she remains silent, compliant, and smiling.

Tina finally arrives at home and rushes through dressing and making up. By 7:30, she's watching the clock, but Ernie still hasn't arrived. At 7:45, fifteen minutes before the party starts, her husband calls: he's tied up having drinks with the boys, he informs her in a slurred voice. He'll try to get there by 9:30. The party is all couples, and Tina is embarrassed to be alone. When she objects, Ernie's belligerent tone shuts her up. Her fears of being by herself are compounded by the memory of the miserable time she had at her sister's party when everyone seemed so much more educated and well off. She had felt tongue-tied and stupid.

Tina's husband never does show up at the dinner party. When she gets home after an exhausting and humiliating evening, he's still not there. After Tina is in bed and almost asleep, Ernie reels in, drunk and demanding sex. Tina is angry and not in the mood, but she's afraid to refuse because Ernie might reject her and seek out another woman. After she heaves a snoring Ernie off her body, Tina finally falls asleep, undoubtably to have another dream of anxiety, embarrassment, and rejection.

A typical day in Tina's life may seem to you comical and far-fetched. This tale may be apocryphal, but it can also be viewed as cautionary. Tina's day is only a slight exaggeration of the scenario that governs many of our lives. Day after day, our time and energy is devoted to the futile search for the right behavior that will ensure we will be liked and approved of. That approval-craving behavior can pollute virtually any and every aspect of our lives, but no one area suffers more from the destructive efforts of obsessive approval-seeking behavior than that of love relationships.

Tina is an extreme example of someone who must have approval in virtually every sphere of her life; she literally contorts herself in an effort to gain everyone's approval and avoid their rejection. Yet many of us engage in much the same behavior to some extent in order to achieve the same goal, particularly with our romantic partners.

Initially, people who seek counseling or therapy rarely present the problem of needing the approval from their partner as an issue they wish to address. In fact, they rarely recognize approval craving or rejection anxiety (its natural corollary) as a problem. This is often because the approval-craving behavior has been occurring for so long it seems a natural and unchangeable part of the personality. Also, to easily admit to the problem would force the approval craver to confront it directly, to risk losing a romantic relationship, and to acknowledge with regret his or her past emotional cowardice as a problem. Therefore, approval cravers come to psychotherapists with other types of complaints.

Pamela came to see me* complaining of pan-anxiety; nameless, vague fears that seemed to overwhelm her. Her symptoms also included hypochondria, sleep disturbances, general malaise, and mild depression. My diagnostic workup revealed that as the wife of a successful banker who was twenty years her senior, she was continually coerced into attending social and business functions she found onerous. Pamela and her husband were childless, and Pamela, who had been a bright and dedicated college student, decided that she wanted to enroll in law school. But her husband wanted her to be available to entertain at home and attend these functions on demand. Most of the people at these functions could have been her parents; the discussions and conversations were stuffy, boring, and totally focused on business. Pamela was a free spirit, a lighthearted person who simply felt suffocated each time she had to attend one of the lengthy, tedious functions in which her husband reveled. He loved to press flesh, to talk with everyone, and to be the last one to leave. Of course, these functions were useful for his business interests, but Pamela's discomfort, anxiety, and feelings of inadequacy would escalate as an evening wore on. She felt estranged from the experience, felt phoney and inauthentic, and, more importantly, felt her time could better be spent by training for a stimulating career in law. Yet she believed that if she did not attend these functions with her husband, he would be deeply disappointed. She would be breaking an unwritten marital contract she had "signed."

*Whenever the first person is used, the reference is to Dr. Lubetkin.

Many women married to successful, driven men share Pamela's feelings. They are pulled along, coerced, and unable to say no for fear of losing their partners. Additionally, they are often made to feel foolish by their partners, who point out, "If you would only relax and enjoy yourself, you would see how nice these people are."

Sarah, a very attractive, thirty-four-year-old housewife, was married to a high-level insurance executive who insisted that she join his weekend golf games with prospective clients and the stuffy elderly executives from his company. Her game was not good, so Sarah's husband insisted that she spend all of her free time working on her game and taking lessons, when she would rather be with her children. Sarah was deeply resentful of this demand, but she was fearful of expressing her feelings in a consistent manner that would lead to change, because she knew that the golf games and the deals her husband clinched on the golf course were so important to him.

Even though it may appear initially that these women had less than valid reasons for doing things they didn't enjoy, this type of compliance—giving in, moving against one's own wishes, and allowing oneself to be controlled time and time again—can be dangerous, emotionally and psychologically. These two women constantly made the excuse to themselves that they "had no other choice." But they did have other choices. They could have directly asserted themselves with their husbands; they could have explained why these activities and behaviors made them unhappy. They could have worked out a compromise arrangement where they participated in these events on a part-time basis, so that they had time to lead their own lives and pursue their own interests. The point is that many women continually give in. A pattern of compliance is established and they begin to lose their own identity very early on in a relationship. Once that process is launched, they tend to get swallowed up almost completely. They rationalize, as these two women did, that if they are to preserve their marriages, if they want to keep the peace, they have to capitulate. But that is usually not the case. Except for the most controlling dictators, most men are willing to make compromises if the women express their needs directly and assertively. That was the problem here:

these two women were unable to express their needs directly and assertively.

In both cases, I worked with Pamela and Sarah to help them express their needs directly. First, we did role playing and rehearsed what they would say to their husbands. We wrote out scripts on cards that they would practice in front of a mirror or with friends or myself. And then they finally confronted their respective husbands with their concerns, and presented alternative possibilities and compromises. In both cases, the husbands were able to make the compromises. But if women do not assert their needs and desires early on in their relationship, a pattern often develops that is extremely difficult to break.

My patients present a wide range of problems in my clinical practice, yet invariably we keep returning to their core belief that their happiness depends on someone else's approval. At least 50 percent of the people seeking psychotherapy today present this problem as a primary or secondary issue. A primary problem is the one people talk about when they first come to see a psychotherapist. The secondary problem is another important issue that gradually emerges after some time in therapy. As noted earlier, approval craving is much more frequently presented as a secondary problem.

Depression, anxiety, phobias, confidence and assertiveness issues, and addictions are often connected to the basic need for the unqualified approval of others and the concomitant terror of rejection. The vast majority of battered and abused wives also report constant worry and striving for their partner's approval. On some level, many of these women even believe they deserve their brutal treatment.

"I'm afraid of what people might think about me," "I don't want to risk losing his love," "I better not make a move unless I'm actually sure," "I don't want to call attention to myself because it might be negative," are common confessions made to me and other psychotherapists. Even fleeting, impersonal relationships can provoke the same catastrophizing thoughts and approval-seeking behavior. The mere thought of returning an item to a store can strike fear in the hearts of those who need and seek universal approval. "What will the salesperson think of me?" such people might agonize. "Am I going to present myself correctly?" "Am I doing this properly?" "Will this salesperson think I'm cheap?"

When asked to monitor their thoughts periodically, approval cravers invariably report surprise at how frequently throughout the day they worry about what people will think of them. They are equally shocked to discover that they seem to be constantly modifying their behavior accordingly. That is, they often find themselves behaving in ways to please or satisfy the needs and desires of others rather than their own.

Try this monitoring exercise yourself. Choose two hours out of your day, and do this exercise several times over the next few weeks. Be sure to have a pencil and paper ready to write down the types of thoughts you are having. Write down your daydreams, your worries and concerns, and your fantasies. Pay particular attention to your thoughts about other people and how you relate to them. When the two hours are up, look over your jottings.

- What are the common themes?
- Does a thread of overconcern for how others view you run through your various thoughts?
- Do worries and fantasies about losing approval pop up with regular frequency?

    Monitor your verbalizations in the same manner during the same time period. Approval craving shows up not just in what you think but in your conversations with others.

- What are the themes of your conversations with people on the job, at the gym, at parties?
- Do you find yourself flattering people inordinately so that they will like you?
- Do you avoid confrontations even if it means allowing your rights to be trampled?
- Do you express doubts about yourself and self-criticism in the hope that others will assure you that you're okay?
- Do you find your conversation focuses on themes of winning the approval of others?
- Is this concern even more exaggerated in your romantic relationship?

If you're truly honest with yourself, you'll find all manner of examples of approval craving in your thoughts and behavior. You might see for the first time that your life is largely focused around this need to have everyone love you.

Approval craving might seem like a strong term, but only a powerful word such as *craving* adequately describes the extraordinary hold this need has on so many people. And the need masks a genuine terror of rejection. Approval craving is an all too common problem in our society. Many, perhaps most of us, *must* have others love us before we can ever begin to like and accept ourselves.

The harmful effects of approval craving manifest themselves in many areas of our lives other than love relationships. For example, some airline accidents have actually been attributed to the junior copilot's reluctance to offend the senior pilot by pointing out his superior's error. The point is that it's virtually impossible to evaluate the cost in terms of human suffering created by this overwhelming need for approval.

Overconcern with others' approval and the accompanying fear of rejection create a life based on a myriad of decisions made strictly according to which one will guarantee the acceptance of everyone—family, friends, lovers, even total strangers. Extreme approval cravers dress to please, talk to please, behave to please, and smile no matter what. They avoid voicing concerns and opinions that might offend, as if a censor is working overtime in their heads, editing and reediting the material they are willing to share with others.

Those who engage in such behavior could be called "chameleons." It is not unusual for women to have dermabrasion, liposuction, breast enlargements, breast reductions, and all manner of cosmetic surgery out of the desire to transform themselves to please someone other than themselves. We are not unalterably opposed to these procedures. (In fact, we endorse any physical and/or psychological changes in a person that enhance self-esteem, as long as their motivation is their *own* desire to look better for themselves and not blind obedience to another's demands.) Unfortunately, a look at the backgrounds of these woman often reveals a long history of various other manifestations of chameleonlike behavior. They generally avoid alienating the people in power by practicing absolute compliance.

"Chameleons" change personality and even appearance constantly, according to the audience of the moment. Eventually they forget who they really are and even disparage the importance of *knowing* who they are. They often lack an inner sense of identity, and any idea of what they truly need. If ever asked directly what they want, chameleons simply blank out and offer little or no response. Of course, their aim—universal approval—is an impossible goal that invariably leads to serious dysfunction.

I often conduct an "I need" exercise with my chameleon patients. I suggest that they sit quietly for a few minutes and think about what they need at that very moment. It could be a need as simple as a hug, a glass of water, or a compliment. Many of these chameleons are so lacking in inner identity and a sense of what they need that they become stuck. They've simply lost the habit of thinking in terms of their own personal needs. Amazingly, some patients have even asked me, "What's the right answer?"

A common example of shaping lives out of the need to be approved of by everyone is seen in men and women who dress and behave in order to present to the world a false image of sexual abandonment. Some women dress provocatively in order to attract men's whistles and other superficial flattery—the illusion of approval—as opposed to seeking a more satisfying and nurturing relationship. I have treated women who would dress and strut for their daily promenade past the same construction site. The whistles and comments were the highlight of the day—a type of fix.

The fact of the matter is that men simply do not spend as much time thinking about how they dress or making themselves up or fixing their hair in order to be provocative and sexual to the opposite sex. This does not mean that men are not concerned about how they look and about the impact they have on women, but the degree to which women will engage in this provocative dressing far surpasses the men. Men may find other ways of being provocative: talking about their money, their power, past conquests. But the focus on physical appearance is still much more the woman's domain.

Doreen, a thirty-two-year-old fashion buyer, would report to me a deep sense of depression after a day during which she did not receive what she considered her due of male attention. On days when she got that attention, when men told her how hot she looked and complimented her on her outfit, she felt light and buoyant, almost giddy with pleasure. Doreen's entire sense of self-worth was tied in with winning approval even though that approval came from complete strangers.

Some women may be offended by anonymous male attention, whereas some of us—men and women alike—may have harmless exhibitionist tendencies. We simply like to show ourselves off. All that matters is whether or not our behavior serves our needs and best interests. Is the attention of men on the street a harmless boost to our self-esteem, or is it providing superficial but necessary reinforcement—a temporary high that shores up a fragile ego? Is this approval far safer than the risk of a deeper relationship that could end in rejection?

Some approval cravers experience what might be termed situation-specific approval needs. Like many of us, they appear unfettered by disapproval fears in most situations, and they genuinely are. But in certain specific situations or with certain specific people, they become overwhelmed with the need to please and be liked.

Connie, a bank loan officer, is extremely assertive on the job. She is never plagued by worries about rejection when she turns down an applicant for a loan. Yet with her steady boyfriend, Ralph, she's a quivering whippet, always hovering about, anxious about pleasing him and anticipating his every whim. If she fails to do so, he might not marry her and she wouldn't be able to find another man.

Situation-specific approval is one of psychology's most amazing phenomena. I'm often stunned by the contrast between the aggressive, confident go-getter in public life, who transforms into a timid, self-effacing, cowering whimp in the presence of her love object.

*No one area of life more glaringly reflects the craving for approval than romantic relationships.* This is because in all other aspects of life—at work, within a social group, even within the family—most of us can take refuge behind a role. In a romantic relationship sooner or later, we are stripped of roles. We are forced to face our partner simply as the woman or man we are—unprotected and vulnerable.

## Why Is This Problem So Universal?

There are several reasons why the obsessive need to be approved of and accepted is so widespread.

♦ *Religious upbringing often instructs us to turn the other cheek, even when that may not be appropriate.*

Violette, a thirty-four-year-old Sunday school teacher, was raised by very religious parents in middle America. She had been taught throughout her life to forgive the sins and transgressions of others, even if they were harmful to her. Her father had been humiliated and insulted for his beliefs, and Violette had witnessed his tolerance of abuse without protest. At home, he would describe these incidents to Violette and her sister, telling the girls he expected them to display the same forgiveness toward others. Whereas this approach may have appeal from a moral point of view, it may not be relevant for twentieth-century New York City, where Violette's dominant and controlling supervisor would confront her on her teaching work in a malicious and humiliating way, suggesting that she was incompetent. Violette would turn the other cheek and suffer in silence even though she recognized the inappropriateness of the supervisor's remarks. Violette's repression had a negative effect on her teaching. After some therapy, though, Violette finally recognized and acted on her right to protest.

♦ *Powerful social pressures that demand we be "appropriate" often cause us to confuse issues of selfishness with those of self-interest.*

Gina, a twenty-four-year-old secretary with a strong religious upbringing, would visit her boyfriend who worked as a bartender at a popular Manhattan singles bar. As she sat on a barstool, she found herself unable to turn away the men who approached her. She would give out her phone number while visiting with her boyfriend because she felt guilty to be in a situation in which men could rightly consider her fair game. She simply could not risk their disapproval by explaining that she was the bartender's girlfriend.

♦ *Poor examples set by parents do not teach children to become assertive and toughen their skins in the face of criticism or disapproval.*

Jane, a forty-year-old housewife, was referred to me by a colleague for assertiveness training. She had been raised by a single mother, who was herself raised in Europe and was now a maid for a very wealthy family in a suburb of New York. As a child, Jane had often worked side by side with her mother, cleaning the house, and had regularly witnessed her mother meekly accepting unfair criticism from her employer. Jane's mother would acknowledge the unfairness of the situation but explain to her daughter that she needed the job and had to put up with the criticism. Whereas the mother's explanations were well meaning, Jane learned from her primary role model to not stand up to unfairness.

♦ *Overcritical or chronically disapproving parents raise offspring who become crippled by an extreme oversensitivity to criticism. This may lead them to devote most of their time and energy to skirting its possiblity. Constant disapproval, criticism, or indifference by a parent or parents in the absence of a real sense of being loved can lead to an endless search for the right formula to gain that withheld approval and love. In cases of emotional or physical abuse, the yearning and the search becomes even more urgent.*

Elaine, a twenty-eight-year-old real estate broker, was successful in many ways. She even remarked to me that she was acting in a "counterphobic way," by working in a field that almost guarantees negative evaluation, as her customers would regularly reject homes and apartments she showed them. Elaine loved her work, yet each time her choice of home for a customer was rejected, she would feel a surge of psychic pain and an additional desire to work overtime to get them to like her and her selection the next time. Elaine would often stay up half the night, scheming ways to please her clients. She was less concerned about their rejection of houses than their acceptance of her; she wanted them to know how hard she was working on their behalf so that they would like her far more than the actual job required. Elaine had grown up in a highly critical household; her mother would squelch her for an endless list of faults. Elaine grew up thinking she could do very little well, and could never find the right formula to please her mother. The mother particularly liked to criticize Elaine for minor faults in front of her friends, so Elaine was reluctant to invite her playmates home after school. Her overcompensation to please her clients was Elaine's indirect response to years of futile attempts to please an implacable mother.

Our relationship with our parents teaches us how to relate to our own adult love partners. If that primal relationship involves some manner of withholding approval, we naturally transfer an inordinate need for approval to our partner.

## *Self-Interest Versus Selfishness*

Of course, it is still appropriate to desire and wish (but never *demand*) that our partner love and approve of us. The goal of this book is not to create personalities who are islands unto themselves—narcissistic fiends who lack all concern about how others view them. But many of us take the need to be loved too far. We obsess about one tiny, insignificant rejection from our partner; we are even haunted by it. Chances are we crave approval in other areas of our lives. A scowl from a stranger on a bus could haunt us for days. "Why me?" we might ask ourselves. "What horrible secret about me did he somehow ferret out? How did I bring that evil look upon myself?"

Being accepted, liked, and loved unconditionally has become far too important an issue in too many lives that have been sacrificed at the altar of someone else's approval. The goal of this book is not to create selfish monsters, but we do want you to recognize that your life should not be devoted to the cause of winning your partner's love and avoiding even the tiniest expression of disapproval at the cost of sacrificing your own best interests.

Also, we want to help you identify the distorted thoughts and behavior patterns that contribute to your exaggerated concern. It is those thoughts that create approval-craving/rejection terror and keep many of us trapped—not only in miserable relationships but in other negative behavior patterns that prevent us from being fulfilled, productive people.

Remember: there really is no such thing as a person who is "too nice." That "nice" person who scrupulously avoids offending her partner may seem to be a miracle of sensitivity and consideration, but, in reality, is simply building a wall of "good acts" and "pleasant expressions" to barricade herself against the overwhelming prospect of disapproval and rejection.

## How Does This Problem Reveal Itself?

Approval craving manifests itself in a broad range of behaviors. It is a fundamental issue that underlies and maintains various other emotional problems grouped under traditional psychiatric diagnostic categories such as depression, anxiety, shyness and unassertiveness, obsessive-compulsive disorder, phobias, relationship communication issues, and addictions. Overconcern for people's approval, particularly that of the love object, is a fundamental issue that can create, feed, and maintain each of these problems.

For example, addictive behavior often results from the addict's attempt to numb himself to the terror evoked by thoughts of rejection. Not surprisingly, addicts are notoriously unsuccessful in their love relationships. Addicts bring an inordinate need for approval to twelve-step programs (Alcoholics Anonymous, Overeaters Anonymous, Narcotics Anonymous, Gamblers Anonymous). Once addicts recognize that they don't have to work so hard for acceptance or run so hard from the prospect of disapproval, they have found an important key toward recovery. In these programs, addicts discover they can talk openly about being an alcoholic or a drug addict—about all the shameful things they have done—and still be accepted. This is very important because not only does the desperate need for approval keep addicts from acknowledging that they have a problem, *it is often the actual basis of the problem*. Addicted people are often so hungry for approval, so filled with a vague but pervasive inner shame and a sense of being unable to handle life's problems, that they turn to an addictive substance or behavior for relief.

The unconditional acceptance that is the spiritual basis of many of these self-help programs can give addicts some of the nurturance they lacked in their early, formative years. This validation of their worth helps them overcome their exaggerated need for approval and enables them to form—often for the first time—a workable relationship with a love partner. In fact, some of the slogans, traditions, and steps of these programs can be understood in terms of strategies to help overcome approval craving.

For example, one of the most powerful experiences one encounters at a twelve-step meeting is reciting the serenity prayer: *God grant me the serenity to accept the things I cannot change, the courage to change the things I can, and the wisdom to know the difference.* The essential message of this prayer from our perspective boils down to, "If I can't get people to love me and approve of me, I will accept it and let it go." Phrases such as "One day at a time" and "Keep it simple, stupid" convey the sense of not complicating your life, not going beyond yourself in terms of relationships. In fact, these programs advise you not to date anyone for at least a year, particularly not anyone in the program. The point is to keep your life as uncomplicated as possible. You need time to thaw out from the numbing effects of your addictive substance or behavior and to explore the approval-craving/rejection anxiety that will surface into consciousness once the addiction pattern has been interrupted.

Despite the help that unconditional acceptance provides the addict in general, self-help groups and therapists often miss the key underlying issue: the *craving* for approval and the terror of rejection it masks. Because these programs and therapists often focus on other symptoms and fail to address this issue systematically and provide a recovery plan, their solutions can be only partial.

Ironically, many approval cravers may seem at first glance to be just the opposite. Many women who appear to be totally oblivious to approval from their partners, who are controlling and abrasive, who engage in testing behaviors, or who are very independent, may actually turn out to manifest the greatest approval-craving/rejection anxiety once their facade is weakened and penetrated. In fact, they are often so terrified of trying to gain approval and failing in the attempt that they mask that need utterly, and do not make an effort at all.

To see whether or not you are disguising your need for approval through a facade of abrasiveness, independence, or indifference, answer the following questions. Be as honest with yourself as possible. No one else ever has to read this!

- Is it important to let your partner think that his evaluation of you is not that crucial?
- Are you often told that you are too controlling of everything that you and your partner do?
- Do you often dress (behave, use makeup) in the opposite way that your partner would prefer or to attract the attention of other men?
- Do you deliberately signal your independence by going out alone even if you don't feel like it, by not telephoning when you should, or other acts that test your partner's loyalty and attentiveness?
- Does your partner accuse you of being abrasive and cold to him?

If you answered yes to these questions, you might be disguising your approval needs under a facade of pseudoindependence and indifference.

Claire would go out to clubs with her boyfriend several nights a week. She was terrified of the attention he generally received from other women, but she disguised her fears by wandering away from him, spending most of the time with friends and other men, and deliberately ignoring him. At all moments, though, her eye was surreptitiously glued on him as her mind raced with anxious thoughts about other women. In a sense, Claire fearfully anticipated losing her boyfriend. Her behavior was designed to protect herself from the hopelessness and despair she feared would overwhelm her if her nightmare was ever realized.

Whether or not your approval craving is apparent to others, in order to once and for all free yourself of your *denial* that you need your partner to approve completely of everything you do, you must do the following:

1. Recognize that you operate from the basic (but erroneous) belief that without that total approval from the love object you are diminished in value.
2. Understand how this basic belief came to be.
3. Realize that maintaining this false belief is your undoing. You are severely limiting yourself and your life's potential.
4. Recognize that this basic belief invariably becomes a self-fulfilling prophecy. The very thing you most fear will surely come to pass.
5. Identify the exact thoughts, feelings, attitudes, fears, and behaviors related to your approval craving.
6. Work dutifully and aggressively to challenge and undercut the irrational thoughts and feelings that have led to your approval craving.

## What This Book Can Do For You

This book has been written from the recognition that thought and behavior are inextricably integrated, and that *real change happens only when both are addressed*. The key to overcoming approval craving, therefore, lies in finding ways to change the faulty thoughts that create the undesirable behavior. This book offers an action plan for change consisting of techniques that combine both cognitive (thought) and behavioral approaches.

We recognize your human fallibility, your tendency to put off making these difficult changes. This book will work with you to help you overcome your long-held beliefs that you must be polite at the cost of sacrificing your self-interest, that you must avoid rocking the boat at all costs, and that you must put others' needs ahead of your own, even to your detriment. This book provides you with the motivation and the skills that empower you to free yourself from your overwhelming need.

Step by step, as you proceed through the exercises and lessons of this book, you will accomplish two objectives.

1. *You will change the beliefs or cognitions* that underlie and fuel your need for general universal approval and your approval craving in romantic relationships, as well as the accompanying terror of rejection.

2. *You will change the behaviors those thoughts cause.* You will be given goals for changing thoughts and behaviors, along with precise instructions on how to achieve these goals. You will be told exactly what risks you have to take. Representative case histories will be described to illustrate how others have already applied these strategies to change their own lives.

## Changing Your Thoughts and Beliefs

In order to change a belief or thought, we offer two classes of solutions. Let's suppose a woman fears that if she should take a night out with her friends, her partner will retaliate in some unbearable manner. He might start a regular habit of going out a few nights a week with the boys, or sulk and make her life miserable or, even worse, find a more compliant woman. This fear causes her to stay at home, to make herself completely available to her partner, and to sacrifice her friendships and outside interests.

The strategic solution—the one that helps deal with a specific situation such as this—involves collecting indisputable evidence that her catastrophizing about the particular anticipated situation is illogical and unnecessary, and is a product of habitually flawed thinking.

The philosophical solution—the one that frees her for the rest of her life—involves attacking the "awfulness" of the worst-case scenario; that is, the worst that could actually happen, even if her partner objected and attempted some sort of retaliation, that the rejection would be terrible and unbearable.

The philosophical is a more elegant solution than the strategic because she arrives at the belief that even if she is rejected, it won't render her helpless—that the disturbance will be temporary and tolerable. Clearly, we would like to move you to arrive at both strategic and philosophical solutions. This book teaches you how to identify flawed thinking and how to use these two classes of solutions to make repairs, corrections, and modifications.

## *Changing Your Behavior*

Restructuring thoughts and beliefs is not enough. To effectively conquer disapproval fears, you must be trained in new self-empowering behaviors. Through appropriate exercises that transform the words of this book into concrete reality, you will learn and rehearse new assertiveness skills. You will be guided through exercises that take you into the world to enact rejection-risking situations involving your relationships with others. Acting out real-life exercises that challenge the belief that rejection from anyone is intolerable further alters your thinking patterns in a positive manner. These shifts in thinking then create additional positive effects on subsequent real-life behavior. And the process continues, as faulty thoughts and behaviors are systematically replaced with more positive, life-fulfilling ones.

The behavioral exercises included in this book's plan for change have three goals.

1. Goal 1 is to teach you to map the life experiences that led to your craving for approval and the fear of rejection from your partner. For example, one client told me at the close of a therapy session, "I understand now why I'm so afraid of falling in love and why I'm so fearful of public humiliation. It's because my mother kept telling me all throughout my childhood that I was no good."

By itself, that insight will not lead to change, but it may be a necessary component in the process. This book provides exercises that take you back in time to key relationships and exchanges with friends and family. These exercises will help you think through those life events that helped create your approval-craving/ disapproval terror.

2. Goal 2 is to teach you to engage in behaviors that reduce inhibitions and rejection anxiety through relaxation techniques, systematic desensitization (exposure to gradually intensifying ideas and images that normally produce anxiety), "flooding" fears of humiliation, and visualization.

3. Goal 3 is to teach you to rehearse behaviors that risk disapproval, such as learning to say no and standing up to your partner. Recall the stories of Tina and Pamela at the beginning of this book. How many of your own thoughts and actions within the context of your love relationship are similarly determined by such overwhelming need for approval? Take this self-test and see. Score 3 points for a response of "always," 2 points for "sometimes," and 1 point for "never."

## Fear of Disapproval Survey

1. Do you often feel grateful that your partner accepts you at all?
   ☐ Always    ☐ Sometimes    ☐ Never
2. Do you hang onto every word your partner says about your future together, as if he is the sole person determining that future?
   ☐ Always    ☐ Sometimes    ☐ Never
3. Do you find that your feelings about yourself improve when your partner seems attracted to you and plummet when he ignores you or seems unattracted to you?
   ☐ Always    ☐ Sometimes    ☐ Never
4. Have you noticed a gradual erosion of your values and preferences in favor of your partner's as the relationship continues?
   ☐ Always    ☐ Sometimes    ☐ Never
5. Have friends regularly commented that you seem to be losing your "self" and are being inordinately influenced by your partner?
   ☐ Always    ☐ Sometimes    ☐ Never

6. Do you regularly find yourself daydreaming about various ways you can avoid your partner's displeasure and win his constant approval?

    ☐ Always    ☐ Sometimes    ☐ Never

7. Does your partner often point out to you that you are letting him take the lead too often in decisions and planning?

    ☐ Always    ☐ Sometimes    ☐ Never

8. Are you usually fearful or intimidated by your partner's displeasures?

    ☐ Always    ☐ Sometimes    ☐ Never

9. Are you regularly editing and censoring your opinions and feelings, particularly if you suspect they will offend or annoy your partner?

    ☐ Always    ☐ Sometimes    ☐ Never

10. Do you find yourself engaging in sexual activities with your partner that you secretly loathe or abhor?

    ☐ Always    ☐ Sometimes    ☐ Never

11. Do you fake orgasm with your partner?

    ☐ Always    ☐ Sometimes    ☐ Never

12. Do you lie or deceive your partner regarding money expenditures, credit cards, and so on, so as not to garner his displeasure, even if your purchases are justified?

    ☐ Always    ☐ Sometimes    ☐ Never

13. Do you often find yourself doing things you really don't want to do because you want to please or satisfy your partner?

    ☐ Always    ☐ Sometimes    ☐ Never

14. Upon meeting a prospective love object, do you work harder than you should to impress him?

    ☐ Always    ☐ Sometimes    ☐ Never

15. Do you find criticism from your partner—even the most constructive advice—difficult to handle, even devastating?

    ☐ Always    ☐ Sometimes    ☐ Never

16. If a restaurant meal is not to your liking, are you reluctant to return it because your partner might become impatient or annoyed?

    ☐ Always    ☐ Sometimes    ☐ Never

17. Would you have difficulty asking your partner to return a loan of money?
    ☐ Always    ☐ Sometimes    ☐ Never

18. Do you worry about letting your partner see you ungroomed and without makeup?
    ☐ Always    ☐ Sometimes    ☐ Never

19. Are you afraid to take off your clothes in front of your lover when the lights are on?
    ☐ Always    ☐ Sometimes    ☐ Never

20. Do you dress to please your partner rather than yourself?
    ☐ Always    ☐ Sometimes    ☐ Never

21. Are you afraid to appear on the beach in a bathing suit because your partner might compare you unfavorably to other women?
    ☐ Always    ☐ Sometimes    ☐ Never

22. If you are in a class or a group of some type, are you afraid to speak for fear of embarrassing yourself in front of your partner?
    ☐ Always    ☐ Sometimes    ☐ Never

23. Are you afraid to go to a party with strangers because your partner might find someone else at the party more attractive?
    ☐ Always    ☐ Sometimes    ☐ Never

24. Are you afraid to introduce your partner to your attractive friends out of the fear that he will prefer them to you?
    ☐ Always    ☐ Sometimes    ☐ Never

25. If you live with your partner, are you afraid to ask for the household funds you feel you require?
    ☐ Always    ☐ Sometimes    ☐ Never

26. Are you afraid to wear a new, eye-catching outfit because your partner might accuse you of being a show-off or find you ridiculous?
    ☐ Always    ☐ Sometimes    ☐ Never

27. Are you afraid to refuse when your partner asks you to do something you feel is illegal, unethical, or simply inappropriate?
    ☐ Always    ☐ Sometimes    ☐ Never

If you scored a total of 54–78, you suffer from an exaggerated need to have your partner approve of you. If you scored 35–54, you undoubtably spend some time performing mental acrobatics in your efforts to gain total acceptance and love from him. If you scored 34 or less, congratulations! Approval craving is not your number one problem.

Keep your score handy. Every few weeks, as you embark on a new phase of your program, retest yourself in order to gauge your progress by your declining scores. So that you can plot and monitor your progress more clearly as you move through the steps of the program, keep a graph of the changes in your scores.

Because we cannot possibly sample every situation that you might recognize as stirring up your approval craving, it might also be useful for you to generate four or five of your own questions that are individualized and specific for your situation. Write them down with your "always," "sometimes," and "never" responses. Notice whether or not your responses to your own, customized questions change over time.

## Getting Past the Stumbling Blocks

After receiving numerous letters following the publication of our book *Bailing Out: The Healthy Way to Get Out of a Bad Relationship and Survive*, it became clear to us that the primary reason the relationships the writers described were unsatisfactory was a lack of assertiveness on the part of one partner and the extraordinary lengths these people would go to please their partners while putting their own needs and desires on hold.

These approval cravers work so hard to avoid any comment or action from their partner that smacks of disapproval or rejection that they devote a good part of their energy and time trying to second-guess that partner's desires until their own lives no longer belong to themselves.

Just as cancer or heart patients are fortunate to live in the 1990s, a decade in which medical technology offers them an unprecedented opportunity to minimize or conquer their disease, so approval cravers can benefit from the last twenty years of developments and improvements in cognitive and behavioral psychology. This book makes use of these developments. If you use it wisely, this book can do many things for you.

In a simple and down-to-earth fashion, this book will teach you to apply the techniques and strategies of cognitive behavioral therapy to overcoming your craving for approval and the fears of disapproval. Many people have paid thousands of dollars in fees to their therapists to learn essentially the same techniques we will teach you in this book. Our eight-step plan for change has been distilled from thousands of psychotherapy sessions with people just like you who have consulted Dr. Lubetkin over the past twenty-two years. In that many of the techniques we use in therapy are out-of-the-office homework assignments that the client does on her own, they have been naturally adapted in the design of this book as a guide—a type of workbook to help you overcome your approval craving by yourself. You can even team up with a buddy and report your experiences to each other, offer each other moral support, and share your successes.

This program will help you attack your resistance, your procrastination, your excuses, and your justifications—the stumbling blocks between you and freedom from the need to be loved unconditionally before you can feel acceptable to yourself.

## The Eight-Step Program

Step 1 will give you an overview of the problem and help you learn exactly what psychological symptoms are created by your problem, and, in turn, what psychological symptoms have created your approval craving.

Step 2 will help you discover how certain life experiences—implicit rules learned early in life that should have been purged years ago—continue to exert a troubling and inhibiting influence. You will track how these rules developed and learn how they connect to your damaging people-pleasing behavior, particularly in love relationships.

Step 3 will teach you to identify and attack the persistent and illogical thoughts and ideas held in common by nearly all approval cravers. You will recognize how you are actually creating your own upsetting feelings about rejection and approval and how you can stop that process dead in its tracks.

Step 4 will teach you how to assess the precise extent of your approval craving, not only in your love relationship but in other spheres of your life: social, work, and family. You will learn special and distinctive techniques that teach you to become a more independent and inner-directed person in each of these areas.

Step 5 will guide you through a profound philosophical change in the way that you value yourself and promote your self-esteem. You will be taught how to finally stop valuing yourself based on *what you do or don't do, or accomplish or don't accomplish*, in your life. You will learn to base your worth on something much simpler and saner. By accomplishing this philosophical shift in your thinking, your vulnerability to disapproval and your obsessive and needless craving for approval can end once and for all.

Step 6 will teach you several powerful behavioral techniques that countercondition your anxiety about rejection and free you from your obsessive worries. All you will need to make these techniques work is twenty minutes a day, a quiet room, a tape recorder, and a good imagination. If you need help with your imagination, we will even show you how to wake it up.

Step 7 will present shame-attack exercises that will teach you to stop feeling irrationally ashamed of anything you do, even if you are totally disapproved of by your partner for some less than commendable act or behavior on your part. If you are like most people, you might bridle and resist these real-life exercises at first. With time, though, you will find them to be among the most helpful exercises in the book. Remember, a fundamental principle to make the change from an approval craver to an independent, assertive person is to *behave* your way into feeling and thinking differently. The exercises in this chapter will help you to do just that.

Step 8 is of particular importance to readers who have children. Part of your own recovery from the insidious problems of approval craving and rejection anxiety involves sharing with others what you have learned. This process will reinforce your own learning. At the same time, it is highly possible that your children want acceptance from others so badly that they may well fall into the same emotional morasses out of which you have just climbed. Here you will find empathetic advice spelled out in step-by-step fashion so that you can help your children.

A final word before you embark on your eight-step journey: The acquisition of any new set of behaviors or skills involved in overcoming your approval craving and disapproval anxiety takes work—hard work! There is no question that when you have completed the eight weeks, life will still be full of hassles—the problems that any active, involved member of society naturally encounters. But if you follow diligently the guidelines described in this book and are patient and tolerant with your own human fallibilities and limitations, you will be rewarded with a freedom from anxiety that had always seemed impossible to achieve. You will like yourself more, no matter what!

After working with this book, you will note the following changes:

- Your opinion of yourself will increase dramatically.
- If your relationship is basically viable, you will deepen the love in the relationship by increasing the mutual love and respect you have for each other.
- If your relationship is no longer viable, you will finally be able to clarify your feelings and do what is best for you.
- You will rid yourself of many other symptoms to which approval cravers are vulnerable.
- You will be able to control anger and outbursts of rage.
- You will be able to assert yourself more positively and with greater ease in many areas of your life.

# APPROVAL CRAVING: THE SYNDROME AND ITS SYMPTOMS

♦

## *What Exactly Is This Problem About:*

Overconcern with approval masks a fear of negative evaluation. Underneath the desire to have everyone like us lies the fear of their dislike. The thought of anyone's disapproval—particularly that of a love object—is frightening, perhaps even terrifying. Any sort of criticism is viewed as so devastating that it may even be experienced as life-threatening. For some approval cravers, even the rejection of total strangers with whom we have no ongoing commitment takes on great importance. Somehow we must get *everyone* to like us, or at least somehow get everyone to not turn against us. Studies have shown that Americans' number one fear is of public speaking. Clearly, that fear is associated directly with the terror of exposing ourselves to the possibility of disapproval. We are afraid of being mocked, laughed at, viewed as trivial, or unattractive.

Stacy, a thirty-four-year-old business executive who had a history of alcoholism, was called on regularly to give presentations at her company. Stacy suffered from the "great imposter" syndrome, which means that she was terrified of being found out as someone who didn't really belong in the responsible position she was in. Stacy felt this way about herself because of her past alcohol problems, even though they were resolved many years earlier. She still felt that somehow she would be exposed as an addictive personality. Stacy was seen as a rising star, but she felt she would be unable to fulfill that expectation because of her intense fear of public speaking, particularly when it came to opening meetings, reviewing the history of the subject under discussion, and formal settings in which chief executives might be present to evaluate her negatively. It turned out that her underlying fear was of being exposed as a reformed alcoholic, that people at the company would be prejudiced against her and consider her unworthy. She had never felt comfortable and accepted, even by those who knew she had recovered from a serious addiction. During a sensitivity training course held at the company, Stacy was finally able to talk openly about her past drinking problems, some of the childhood traumas that had probably set the stage for her alcoholism, and her fears of being discriminated against by the teetotalers at the company and others who simply did not understand the nature of alcoholism. From that point on, Stacy felt much more comfortable about delivering speeches. She no longer feared that words would freeze in her mouth and that people would mock her as an imposter.

Social evaluative anxiety and unassertiveness are extremely important problems people bring to therapy.

Winning the approval of others and avoiding their rejection is such a prevalent issue for so many that they simply accept the need for approval as part of their psyches. Many people tell themselves,

"I don't think I could ever change that. It's the way I am. I care too much about what other people think of me."

But this way of thinking and the behavior it creates can be changed!

Some people tell themselves that to not concern themselves with the approval of others is to be arrogant, narcissistic, and self-serving. Or they maintain that there is nothing wrong with needing everyone to like them. But it is surely wrong if this need interferes with functioning. The key to understanding how approval craving interferes with normal functioning is to ask what underlies it. Do fear and guilt underlie this need to have people like you? Or are you really caught up in the spirit of giving; do you really love people and want to nurture them? The point is that not everyone who works hard to get others to like her is victimized by fear and guilt. Approval craving is destructive only if it's not serving your best interests.

Rene volunteers her time at a hospital. It's very important to her that the patients like her, care about her, trust her, and feel comfortable with her. Rene's need to be liked is not necessarily underscored by fear and guilt. It's just a genuine desire to reach out to people and have them feel she is good to them. Her impulse to be liked stems from humanistic and spiritual concerns.

For some people, however, concern with other people's approval, in their own minds at least, seems to serve other, overriding purposes. They may have made money because they've been polite and appropriate. Their success in their careers may be a result of learning how to be compliant. If so, approval seeking may not be an issue. The point is, does their behavior serve their self-respect?

Sylvia worked hard to keep her boss happy. But she developed an ulcer that her doctor informed her was stress-related. In therapy, she finally learned that the reason for her stress and subsequent illness was all of the overtime work she did in pleasing her boss—making sure he liked her. Clearly, she was successful at her career, but the success was purchased at too high a cost.

If your self-respect is suffering as a consequence of overconcern with others' approval, you're in trouble. This is particularly true if this craving for approval rules your behavior in love relationships—the one area of life in which you should feel free to be most authentically yourself.

## Questions Concerning Approval Craving

♦ *How many people suffer from approval craving?*

Approval craving is a universal experience. I have never met a human being who, upon questioning and honest answering, does not admit that at some point or points in his or her life, or with some people in his life, he or she has felt a strong need to be liked or approved of. The real issue, of course, is not whether or not this problem is universal, but how it impacts on any one person's ability to function happily. Therefore, the degree to which you crave approval determines how destructive it is. The distinction, then, is a matter of severity and degree. In an informal survey of my patients and other patients who had been treated at the Institute for Behavior Therapy, close to 75 percent of those asked reported that they suffer from a moderate to severe degree of approval craving. In the nonpsychiatric population—that is, those who have not chosen to seek out help or who do not need help—that number is undoubtedly quite lower. However, it should be pointed out that mild or moderate levels of approval craving that go untreated or unmonitored can deteriorate, as the person has more and more life experiences, into a more severe approval-craving.

♦ *Is approval craving normally a lifelong problem, or do people lapse in and out of it?*

The answer to this question is largely determined by other psychiatric or emotional problems that people have. Often, depressed patients will feel much more dependent and needy of approval when they are in the midst of a depression. When they come out of it, and they feel more independent and autonomous, they naturally do not manifest the approval-craving problem as severely. The same could be said for people who are anxious. When they are under great stress and experiencing powerful psychosocial stresses in their lives—such as an upcoming marriage, or a job change or location change—they may manifest much more severe forms of approval craving than when their lives are relatively calm, uneventful, and uncomplicated. People can lapse in and out of approval craving, but this is largely determined by other stressors, both internal and external, that are operating simultaneously in their lives. Even people who are in therapy for this problem for an extended period will sometimes lapse in and out of approval craving as their therapy uncovers issues that empower them for a while, only to have some stressor in their lives overtake them.

♦ *Are there occasions when approval craving strikes hardest?*

Again, the answer to this question is related to other, ongoing psychological stressors in a person's life. Approval craving takes on a particularly severe dimension when a person who is fearful of rejection is rejected or abandoned by another significant person in his or her life, or when someone who is very dependent on parents or siblings has to deal with their abandonment. Another example is when a person who has accomplished or gained a good deal in his or her career is challenged on the basis of his or her intellectual ability, or some other ability this person has prided himself or herself on and from which his or her entire sense of self is constructed. In such cases, the person will experience a disruption of that overall sense of self and the criticism is experienced as devastating, thereby instigating a period of severe approval craving.

♦ *What percentage of women suffer from significant approval craving?*

About 80 percent of the patients in therapy who present approval craving as a serious problem are women. This number is skewed somewhat because many more women than men present themselves for therapy. In addition, men are often more reluctant to present this as a problem than are women. However, many more women than men seem to suffer from approval craving. It is also important to point out here that a number of the psychiatric diagnoses in the *Diagnostic and Statistical Manual of Mental Disorders,* better known as DSM3R, are much more common and prevalent for women than they are for men.

For example, one of the primary personality disorders is called *dependent personality disorder.* It is much more prevalent in women than in men. The manner in which this diagnosis is made, according to the DSM3R, is that the patient must demonstrate a number of different behaviors, beginning by early adulthood and present in a variety of contexts. These include the following: "is easily hurt by criticism or disapproval," "is frequently preoccupied by fears of being abandoned," "feels devastated or helpless when close relationships end," "feels uncomfortable or helpless when alone and goes to great lengths to avoid being alone," "volunteers to do things which are unpleasant or demeaning in order to get other people to like her," and so on. The point is that this very prevalent personality disorder, which mainly strikes women, reveals approval craving as a crucial aspect in its diagnosis. Dependent personality disorder is a severe emotional problem, but even if we look at less severe problems such as simple social phobias, we see approval craving manifesting itself.

The prevalence of simple phobias is common in the general population. According to the DSM3R, the essential feature of the simple social phobia is a persistent fear of a certain social situation or embarrassment in certain social situations. The fear is always there that they may do something or act in a way that will be humiliating or embarrassing in a public situation. This disorder, which is much less severe and much more common than dependent personality disorder, is also much more frequently diagnosed in females. Therefore, it is safe to conclude that women are much more vulnerable to approval craving, both in its severe forms, such as dependent personality disorder, and in its more benign forms, such as simple social phobia. It should also be added here that women seem to be socialized more to be concerned about appearance and about what others think of them. Until recently, women were defining their value more in terms of whether or not a man accepted and approved of them. For all of these reasons, women suffer from approval craving far more than do men.

♦ *How many people suffer from mild forms of approval craving but don't necessarily need to consider it a problem?*

In that the phenomenon is almost universal, the answer is that millions experience mild forms of approval craving but don't consider it a problem and never present themselves for therapy. Why? Because it is not a major interference in the important aspects of their lives: financial, academic, career, social, and emotional. They have a nodding awareness that they may be more concerned about people liking them than perhaps they ought to, but it is a low priority item for most of this group. In addition, such people are able to just laugh it off. They are able to kid one another about wanting someone to like them or asking someone for reassurance. But again, they are able to generally treat the matter with levity rather than with great seriousness because it doesn't impact their lives that much.

♦ *Aren't there people for whom this problem is absolutely critical, who are so crippled by approval craving that they are unable to function in life?*

The answer to this question is yes. People with personality disorders such as dependent personality disorder are among the most serious cases in psychiatry. It should be noted that when personality traits are inflexible and maladaptive and cause significant impairment or distress, they become personality disorders. This should not be confused with depression or major depressive illnesses, which fall under a separate category, and, while severe, usually remit after a while. The personality traits discussed here are enduring patterns of perceiving and relating to the environment and oneself. These personality disorders are exhibited in a wide range of significant social and personal situations.

♦ *How many people should seek outside help, and when is outside help to be recommended?*

The answer is simple: anyone who finds that his or her approval craving is interfering with social, academic, economic, or interpersonal functioning. That is, approval craving is causing grief, pain, shame, and embarrassment on an ongoing basis. Such persons should seek out help. Of course, the decision is an individual one. But, if on a daily basis you find yourself frequently overconcerned about the opinions of others, if you find in your relationship that most of your thoughts are peppered with concerns about "am I impressing him?," "Is he going to like me tomorrow?," and so on, then clearly such frequency and intensity of these concerns has to be interfering with your free functioning in the relationship and in your life.

This is similar to defining alcoholism. For years, the questions were: How do you define alcoholism? Is it physiological? Is it psychological? The general thinking now is that if the use of alcohol interferes with one's economic, academic, career, interpersonal, or emotional functioning, then one has a problem with alcohol. It's the same situation with approval craving.

♦ *What should the success rate be for those who use this book?*

Nearly everyone who reads the book and follows the exercises should improve to some degree. We are presenting some of the cutting-edge interventions available for approval cravers. Of course, whereas some readers may improve a great deal, others may improve only minimally and will need to seek out additional professional help. It should be pointed out that sometimes reading a self-help book such as this heightens the reader's awareness of her problem. You are thinking about your approval craving much more than you did previously. You are no longer sticking your head in the sand; and very often, this greater awareness causes you to be even more of an approval craver initially, as you focus on the problem. However, this experience is usually very limited, and after a few weeks of working on the program, you begin to see a decrease in approval-craving behaviors.

♦ *Are there any statistics on the success rate of people who get professional help?*

The answer is a qualified no, in that approval craving itself is such a pervasive problem and occurs in so many different pyschiatric and psychological diagnostic categories. As we noted earlier, no one has taken a good look at the types of changes that take place in terms of statistics. However, we do know that a large number of individuals—probably close to 80 or 90 percent—who have assertive deficits and enroll in some type of assertiveness training program do report mild to marked improvement. This is demonstrated in a number of studies published over the years in such journals as *Behavior Therapy, Behavior Therapy and Experimental Psychiatry,* and *Behavior Research and Therapy.* The types of cognitive behavioral interventions now available can provide help to the vast majority of people seeking assistance. Obviously, the success rate tends to decrease with the complexity of the problem. The more psychological problems an individual has, the more there is to work on and the lower the overall success rate. But with people who present approval craving and assertiveness difficulties as fairly isolated issues, the success rates are very high for either mild to marked improvement.

◆ *Are there special places for people who want or need outside help?*
Absolutely. In nearly every community there are numerous cognitive behavioral therapists who run specialized groups—as well as individual sessions—for assertiveness training and for overcoming interpersonal social anxiety and shyness. These therapists are psychologists, psychiatrists, and social workers. Many of these therapists have identified themselves with one of the major national associations, the primary one being the Association for the Advancement of Behavior Therapy (A.A.B.T.) at 15 West 36th Street in New York City. Anyone can receive a list of practicing cognitive behavior therapists in their community merely by writing the A.A.B.T.

Little evidence exists that other approaches such as acupuncture, Rolfing, Primal Scream Therapy, and so on, can make much of a difference. This is because such techniques don't focus on changing basic belief systems and on teaching new skills as does the cognitive behavior therapy approach.

How pervasive is your approval craving in other spheres of your life? As you look through your answers to these questions, be honest with yourself. Find the patterns in your own behavior.

## On the Job

◆ *Do you behave in an inappropriately compliant manner with your boss?*
Judith reported to me that whenever she had to ask a favor of her

boss, she developed a little-girl voice and behaved in a coquettish, sweet, childish manner. She was disgusted with herself, but found she automatically lapsed into this behavior whenever she placed herself in that dependent situation. When we reviewed her history, we discovered that her childish, submissive behavior had always ensured that her father and older brother would approve of and attend to her.

◆ *Have you slipped into workaholism in order to assure acceptance?*
Donna worked from eight in the morning until seven in the evening, long after everyone at the office had left. Despite the positive feedback she consistently received from her co-workers, she continued to feel terrified at the thought of leaving anything undone for the day or letting anything pile up. She spent far too much time writing long, perfectionistic memos and working over-long hours to ensure acceptance. Donna grew up with a father who pushed her educationally and intellectually and paid attention to and praised her only when she was meeting the exceptionally high standards he had set for her. Not surprisingly, she carried this pattern into her adulthood.

◆ *Do you engage in backstabbing or scapegoating of other, more vulnerable workers in order to enhance your position?*
Danielle was a salesperson who continually backstabbed others to look better in her boss's eyes. Her behavior was both subtle and blatant. She would call her boss's attention to the fact that she topped the sales list. She embarrassed fellow workers at a staff meeting by alluding to their failures. She once noticed an important list of contacts on a fellow worker's desk and actually "misplaced" them. Danielle often reminded her fellow workers of their errors and that she led them in sales. She tried to be charming, but her behavior was clearly designed to enhance her position because she was terrified of failing and being disapproved of. Danielle would do whatever she could to stay at the top of the heap.

◆ *Do you experience inappropriate levels of anxiety when asking for raises or any other reasonable work requests?*
Sandra would come in for extra doses of relaxation training when she knew she had to confront her boss with a work-related request

such as a raise. She would visually anticipate him turning her down, certain that he would even mock her for making the request. She actually once dreamed about her boss saying, "Are you kidding me? Do you really think you deserve this? You have some nerve coming here, given your poor performance at your job."

## With the Family

♦ *Are you still overly compliant to a parent, perhaps to compensate for the perceived favoritism of a sibling? Are you working overtime to win that love?*

Often younger siblings feel that they are playing catch-up their entire lives, attempting to match pace with a favored sibling. They are constantly looking for the formula that will get the parent to favor or appreciate them. From early childhood, Bea spent years catering to her distant, reclusive, emotionally ungenerous father, who worshipped Bea's older brother. The father hardly talked to her, and never asked how she was feeling, but Bea was totally enamored with him and would spend countless hours with him when she was a little girl—going with him to the barbershop or helping him do chores around the house. Bea was always there, waiting for him to give her the approval, attention, warmth, and emotional connectedness he was never able to. When he died two years ago, she was overwhelmed with serious panic attacks. It was almost as if her purpose in life—her fulltime job of getting her father to attend to her and love her—was no longer necessary. She had lost her life's work and was cast adrift.

♦ *Do you make decisions based on what your parents want you to do?*

Some people have to check in with their parents, even as adults, to get their blessing on virtually all decisions. Laura, forty-three, was hysterical about buying a co-op apartment. She had to call her mother every step of the way, getting her advice about mortgages and rates and decorating. Laura hated herself for doing this, knew she was acting like an oversize baby, but felt she could not control her behavior. At bottom, Laura was afraid of risking her mother's disapproval. Her mother was a critical parent who set very high standards for both herself and Laura, and Laura simply did not want to let her down.

♦ *Do you find yourself doing something you don't want to simply because a family member expects it of you?*

Lanie's mother recently died. Her older male cousin—a highly regarded member of the extended family—was so intimidating to her, and Lanie so concerned that he like and approve of her, that she acceded to his requests regarding a headstone and funeral arrangements for her own mother!

## In Social Situations

♦ *Are you afraid of being rejected by strangers who may find your behavior odd and inappropriate? Are you afraid you will feel humiliated?*

These people are called "shy" by others; they are overly concerned with not appearing inappropriate. Cynthia, a tall, willowy beauty, was constantly berated for her posture as a young girl and was teased a good deal because she was so tall and slim. Today, whenever she is in a social situation, she imagines herself to be a strange, giraffelike creature. "Giraffe" was her childhood nickname, and despite her adult attractiveness, she still sees herself as overly tall and awkward.

♦ *Do you avoid approaching people who might be desirable to meet because you are convinced they will not find you acceptable?*

Many people are convinced they are boring and cannot make good conversation. Diane was convinced that her conversation was tedious. Wherever she went, she believed the conversation of others was far more intelligent and insightful. She was terrified of having nothing to say, of her ineptitude at small talk, and of her inability to make transitions from one topic to another. Therefore, she avoided all sorts of social situations because she had convinced herself she would be rejected.

♦ *Do you numb yourself through the use of alcohol or another drug in potentially uncomfortable social situations?*

Alcohol and other drugs accomplish a number of objectives for the approval craver. They temporarily reduce fear and give the feeling that their humor is sharper. Alcoholics and drug users regularly report that when high they are much funnier, more attractive, and socially more appealing. However, when an experiment was set up in which these people viewed videotapes of themselves under the influence in social situations, they realized that they were far less attractive when high. One's wit and sense of humor suffers after several drinks. The perception of your behavior when you're high differs radically from the actuality.

♦ *Are you inappropriately gushy—too open, too soon with new acquaintances?*

The "skin of the onion" principle operates here. The appropriate way of relating to other people is as if you were peeling away the skin of an onion, one layer at a time, removing the outer to approach the inner. Both parties gradually open up to each other. You first talk about the weather and other superficial topics. Later on, you may share something more personal. The next time you meet, you may probe deeper layers, until, finally, several contacts later, you share personal and important material about your dreams, aspirations, concerns, fears, and so on.

Approval cravers frequently believe that if they open up quickly and gushingly, the other person will either feel sympathy and compassion or will be impressed by the show of openness. *This is really a ploy to avoid rejection.*

Janet, a thirty-two-year-old hotel executive was so worried that her dates would reject her that she would share inappropriate information with the man immediately. She would gush about her therapy, her previous heartbreaks, her unhappy childhood. She thought these confidences would align the man on her side. More importantly, she was attempting to control what she assumed would turn out to be a rejection anyway somewhere down the road. She protected herself against this inevitable rejection by giving the man so much information about herself that when he did drop her she could comfort herself by saying, "I know why he rejected me. Once again, I gushed too much."

## With Friends

♦ *Do you make yourself look bad if you feel a friend is jealous of something you have?*

Many people put themselves down and cast themselves in an unfavorable light if they suspect that a friend or acquaintance may be jealous of them. Janet, a forty-one-year-old housewife, was wealthy, but suffered feelings of guilt because she was more well off than her friends. She would put herself down as a useless home-body, often inappropriately, whenever friends commented about her beautiful clothes, jewelry, crystal, and other possessions that signaled her affluence. She had to be taught in therapy how to feel proud and comfortable with what she had accomplished and possessed, and not to automatically assume that others were jealous. Even if they were, that was no reason to humble and humiliate herself in order to insulate herself from their possible disapproval.

♦ *Do you constantly compare yourself unfavorably to your friends?*

This is a corollary of the previous trait. You assume that your friends will humiliate or humble you or disapprove of you, so you compare yourself negatively to your friends.

Iris, a fifty-year-old bookkeeper, would regularly put herself down when she was out with friends. No matter what the situation, Iris would try to convince her friends that she would be the only one who wouldn't meet a man that night, that her clothes were inappropriate, or that she lacked their intelligence and personability. It was as if she were arming herself against the inevitable disapproval she expected from her friends. The rationale was something along the lines of, "If I put myself down aloud and in public, letting you know how little I think of myself, then you are less likely to put me down." If someone else had been mouthing the insults, it would have hurt more.

♦ *Are you afraid to ask a friend to return a loan?*

Are you afraid to ask a friend to return the money because you don't want your friend to consider you miserly or demanding? Even though asking for your money back may be a legitimate request in the context of the relationship, you would rather lose the money than lose face.

Zena, a forty-four-year-old assistant librarian, was underpaid and struggled to make ends meet. But when fellow workers came to her for loans of money, she would invariably respond out of her feelings of inadequacy and her need to be liked and respected. By the time she came to therapy, she had lost well over nine hundred dollars in loans that were not returned. Zena had been too fearful to risk dislike by asking for the money.

♦ *Are you afraid to tell a friend about what you really think of their inappropriate behavior toward you?*

Approval cravers don't want to comment on inappropriate behavior from a friend. They tell themselves, "I'll play it down; it's not that important. I don't want to hurt her feelings and risk even more rejection." I've had patients who've put up with awful abuse from friends and acquaintances, all the while steadfastly refusing to give that person any feedback.

Stephanie, for example, was enamored with a friend who seemed, in Stephanie's mind, to have it all. Stephanie was twenty-five and struggling through college. Her friend was twenty-seven, married to a successful attorney, and quite abusive to Stephanie. She would humiliate Stephanie in front of others, acting as if Stephanie was a dizzy, dumb blonde. Stephanie would simply swallow her pain.

♦ *Are you uncomfortable about turning a friend into a lover because you are sure he will reject you?*

You may have a close relationship with a man who is loving, caring, and nurturing, but the relationship is platonic. You may simply be afraid of seducing this friend or suggesting the two of you move the relationship into a physical relationship, even though you're convinced he's the right guy for you. But he's never made a pass, so you automatically assume he doesn't find you desirable. You never consider that he may be shy, afraid of rejection himself, or the numerous other reasons why he has not initiated a romantic overture.

Sandra, forty, had enjoyed a wonderful platonic relationship for a number of years with Jim, two years her junior. She never indicated in any way that she also harbored a deep physical affection for him. She fantasized about making love with him, but would never take the risk of exposing herself. The years slipped by as Sandra engaged in a number of unfulfilling sexual relationships with other men. After therapy, she learned to take the risk of letting Jim know how she felt, and the relationship finally developed into something wonderful and loving. The last I heard, they were engaged to be married.

## *Primary Psychological Symptoms Associated with Approval Craving*

Consider the following diagram. It pictures most of the primary symptoms related to approval craving. Notice that each of the symptoms simultaneously *creates* approval craving and *results from* approval craving in a continuous feedback loop. Therefore, to overcome approval craving and its destructive effects, you must work to interrupt this dynamic process at any point in the cycle. For example, by overcoming low self-esteem (see Chapter 5), you will control your approval craving. *And* by working directly on your approval craving, you will increase your self-esteem!

Not every approval craver is going to go through each of these symptoms. As a matter of fact, the majority of the approval cravers I work with demonstrate only one or two of these symptoms. Therefore, their feedback loops would be much smaller circles. However, for purposes of simplicity, we are listing in this diagram all of the symptoms associated with the approval-craving syndrome. Look at this diagram and focus on the one or two primary symptoms that you can easily identify in your life. It is a rare person indeed who will go through all of these symptoms. We have listed them all here so that you can easily recognize the symptoms that are plaguing you.

Of course, this is a very generalized guide. In some cases, the symptoms caused by approval craving lead to increased approval

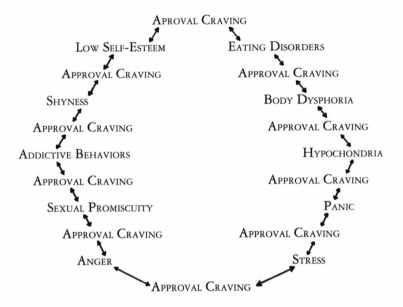

craving. But a depressed person may have worn herself out by her approval-craving behavior, and the process may stop right there.

Look at the diagram carefully and choose the symptoms (there may be only one or two) that seem to predominate for you. You might want to draw your own individualized diagram so that you will have a clear, graphic representation of how your approval craving leads to symptoms that lead to more approval craving, which leads to more symptoms. By creating your own individual diagram you can better keep track of your progress in overcoming this problem.

♦ *Low self-esteem*

Although this is an overused phrase, it simply means an individual who does not esteem or value herself. Her opinions, her judgments, her body, her intellect—her very being—have little or no value. Such people frequently shy away from any situation, work or social, in which they are likely to be rejected or disapproved of by another.

♦ *Shyness and unassertiveness/social phobias (fear of humiliation in public settings)*

These traits seem to be primarily caused by fear of negative evaluation. Shyness and unassertiveness are among the most prevalent problems presented in therapy. These individuals are convinced they will be evaluated negatively by others if they assert themselves, if they open up conversations, if they attempt to make friends, or if they put themselves forward at all.

Denise, a twenty-nine-year-old receptionist, had been extremely shy all of her life. She was often fearful of expressing any opinions or judgments, particularly to strangers or new people in her life. She was shy at parties, and felt extremely uncomfortable around people she didn't know. She was lonely, dejected, and isolated from others. But Denise's shyness and the separation it created also increased her need for approval from others. The more isolated she felt, the more she felt the need to be approved of by someone—anyone. At the same time, she grew increasingly concerned that nobody would ever like her, and that made her even more paranoid about being rejected.

♦ *Alcohol and drug abuse*

The lack of approval tends to lead the person to drink or use other drugs in order to numb the pain and discomfort she experiences. Clearly, these substances cause the person's behavior to be so inappropriate that it guarantees they will lose the approval of others.

Betty had been drinking regularly for a number of years. She'd grown up in a family with hypercritical parents who never appreciated her accomplishments or told her they loved her, and they tended to favor other siblings. In order to gain acceptance with a crowd of acquaintances, Betty began to drink more and more. The drinking gave her a false sense of security with this crowd, but it led to behaviors that caused her to be rejected by these same people she so very much wanted to be approving of her. She would become loud, obnoxious, and angry. She was stuck in a feedback loop: fear of disapproval led to drinking that numbed the pain but led to behavior guaranteed to bring rejection and disapproval, which, in turn, created the need to numb the pain even more.

◆ *Depression*

Martin Seligman's *Learned Optimism* describes a study in which he enclosed dogs in a cage wired with an electrical grid. He shocked them repeatedly and didn't allow them to escape. In the second experiment, the dogs were allowed to escape; that is, a partition separating the wire cage from an unwired cage, was lowered. Time after time, the dogs refused to jump to the safe area. It was as if they had learned to be helpless by being shocked over and over in the past with no chance of escape. Now that escape was actually possible, they simply did not take advantage.

This notion of learned helplessness has been used to explain depression in many people. When individuals such as Yvonne, a thirty-three-year-old homemaker, are depressed, we have to examine the possible causes. Yvonne had learned to be helpless. No matter how hard she worked in the home, attending to her children and her husband Frank's needs, he never gave her the approval she craved. Over time, she grew more and more depressed, as she felt more and more unable to find the formula to make Frank appreciate and love her as she desired. She became progressively more despondent and isolated, which led to a further withdrawal of whatever meager attention her husband and other friends and family members had been giving her. Their withdrawal further confirmed Yvonne's notion that she was unworthy of esteem, love, and acknowledgment, and she became even more depressed.

◆ *Sexual promiscuity*

Sexual promiscuity also creates an endless feedback loop. Many women feel that the only way to gain approval, particularly from men, is to be sexual. For many women this is the one and only guaranteed way for men to attend to them. Even though they may realize intellectually that their entire being is not being appreciated—only their sexual abilities—they are so hungry for any type of approval that they are willing to put up with a hollow victory.

Stockton was such a woman. A stockbroker in her early forties, she'd never been married. She would usually sleep with a man on the first date, and often never see him again. When she entered therapy, we explored the fact that she always felt needy of male approval, that she needed a man to truly lust after her and to make her the center of his world, if only for a night. She would get insanely jealous if the man would look at or talk to another woman or speak of previous girlfriends. She had recognized early in each relationship that the way to ensure at least some absolute attention was to be as sensual and sexual as possible. She'd studied all the books on how to please a man, dressed very provocatively, and engaged in all sorts of fantasy and role-playing with her men—all in order to keep them interested. Stockton was typical of promiscuous women in that she didn't feel much sexually herself. In a very real sense, the sexual feelings such women should be having tend to die off and are replaced by anger and bitterness because at some level they recognize exactly what they are doing. They become numb and often fake orgasm, as Stockton did, but they feel addicted to making sure that men find them attractive and approve of them. In Stockton's case, we could trace the beginnings of her approval needs to her family, especially her father, who was usually on the road. When he was home, he virtually ignored her and tended to deflate her whenever he could.

♦ *Overcompliance in lovemaking*

There are many other ways in which approval-addicted women get into difficulty in terms of their sexuality. Some women will engage in practices they do not desire. Many patients have reported to me that in order to keep a man interested they have engaged in activities that offer little or no pleasure to themselves. Sometimes they have even engaged in activities they find disgusting or reprehensible, but which they knew gave their partner pleasure, and so they elected to engage in them. Many of these women deluded themselves into believing that if they could demonstrate to the man how giving and sexually generous they were, that would somehow guarantee an ongoing commitment from the man to the relationships.

The list of behaviors such woman have engaged in without receiving pleasure themselves is very long indeed. It includes such things as engaging in various role plays with a man that were felt to be "kinky" or too experimental; engaging in various types of lovemaking or positions that were uncomfortable or felt weird to the woman; dressing up in ways that made them feel silly, comical, or uncomfortable, particularly women who feel that sexy clothing made them look foolish; oral sex (both giving and receiving), and engaging in threesomes with another man or woman.

I am reminded of Madge, a thirty-two-year-old executive secretary with a real estate firm, who found herself on several occasions going along with her boyfriend's desires to have another woman join them in bed. She had never done this before, and whereas she did find it mildly exciting, it really was inconsistent with her principles and morals. She also did not like the idea of sharing her boyfriend with another woman, did not find herself particularly attracted to the other woman, and did not want to be exposed to homosexual behavior. And yet, in order to hold onto this man, she would give in each time he suggested it, telling herself that basically it was an innocent behavior, he enjoyed it, and why should she be such a stick-in-the-mud? It was only in therapy that she recognized she was being unassertive, that her needs were not being met and that she was devoting herself far too much to taking care of his desires.

Many approval-craving women focus so much on their partner's pleasure that they exclude their own, to the extent that they don't even know what gives them pleasure. This is an important point. I've often suggested to patients that good sex is selfish sex. That's a direct follow-up to many suggestions made by Masters and Johnson and Helen Singer Kaplan in their classic books on human sexuality. The point is to make certain that you understand that much of your own sexual pleasure takes place in your head and in your body and that you have to be aware of what turns you on and what gets you off in order to fully and completely enjoy the sexual act and to be a good partner to the person you are with. By selfish sex, we mean taking a thorough, complete, and honest assessment of what excites you.

We often do this when doing a sexual assessment of men or women who have sexual problems. We ask them questions such as

What are the fantasies you masturbate to?, What is the type of erotic literature you like?, When you are watching an X-rated movie, what do you zero in on?, When you are with your partner, where is your fantasy?, Do you drop all of your masturbatory fantasies or do you use them to get yourself even more aroused?, How do you like to be touched and stroked—with what speed and what intensity?, and Do you like your genitals or another part of your body touched in a certain way? The list goes on and on. The point is that you need to make a fearless inventory of exactly what excites and arouses you. Lonnie Barbach's *For Yourself* is a good place to begin in assessing exactly what turns you on. Sometimes women have to experiment by themselves, through masturbation and the use of various sexual toys, to become comfortable with knowing what excites them. It is only then that they can fully and comfortably give themselves to a sexual relationship. This is particularly true of unassertive or overly compliant women who can very easily forget about what pleasures they need and become almost entirely tuned in and committed to giving pleasure to their partner to the total exclusion of their own needs.

Unfortunately, there are many partners who will take advantage of this compliance. Either these men are not skilled lovers themselves or they simply have no interest in taking care of their partner's needs.

### ♦ *Sexual aggressiveness as a cover-up for fear of rejection*

Stockton, described in a previous case, displayed this symptom of approval craving. Just as some people who are afraid of public speaking will rally themselves and become superb public speakers to overcompensate for their fears—just as people suffering other types of phobias will engage in counterphobic behavior in order to overcome their fears—such overcompensatory behavior is sometimes seen operating in women who are approval addicts, particularly those afraid of rejection from boyfriends or husbands. The behavior is often acted out as sexual aggression. They will often, as Stockton did, read everything they can get their hands on about giving sexual pleasure. Whereas on the surface they appear to be perfectly wonderful sexual partners, underneath often lies tremendous sexual insecurity. As they continue to flaunt themselves sexually, they are in fact extremely insecure and terrified of being rejected sexually. These are often the people who, if there is any criticism of their behavior or performance in the bedroom, however mild or minute, tend to panic and either overreact by becoming either more sexual—the attitude being, "I'll show him I can perform as well as anyone"—or become defensive and withdrawn and shut down almost completely.

The bedroom is probably a prime battleground in this continuing conflict of personalities. You must be fearless and honest in your own review of your sexual activities. Are you, in fact, falling into one of the traps we have detailed here? If so, it's even more motivation for you to continue reading on, because the exercises presented in this book to help you to overcome your approval craving will help you improve your enjoyment of your sex life by making you much more authentic and communicative in the bedroom. The keys for many of those whose approval craving disrupts their sexual pleasure are honest communication, sharing exactly what you like and don't like with your partner, never being afraid or ashamed of expressing a desire, and never withholding your feelings if something is a turnoff.

◆ *Anger that seems to come from nowhere*

We see this unexplained rage often with approval cravers. When you walk around craving something throughout the day and it's never attained, it's easy to become angry and paranoid, to blame the world.

Charlotte reported to me early in the course of therapy that she felt angry at least once a day. The anger would strike from nowhere, like a bolt of lightning. When we analyzed the thoughts and feelings that preceded the anger, it became clear that in every instance the anger was preceded by thoughts of inadequacy, of not being good enough, of wanting to be loved by someone, or of being abandoned or rejected by others. Once she made this connection between her neediness, approval craving, and her anger, Charlotte's therapy proceeded quickly.

◆ *Phobias and feelings of panic*

Approval cravers often report phobias, feelings of panic, or anxiety that seem to appear from nowhere. We believe that this primarily originates from not feeling a sense of mastery over life's problems. Because they are not getting what they believe they need in terms of affection and approval, and continue to feel needy a great deal of the time, approval cravers often feel so out of control that situations that would hardly disturb the rest of us become imbued with great risk and menace.

Patricia, a thirty-five-year-old executive secretary, came to me complaining of an airplane phobia. When I asked her about parallel life events (what had been going on at the time the phobia developed), she remarked that she had been dropped by a man she'd been going with and obsessed with for a number of years. It was almost as if the moment she felt out of control, unable to get her fix of approval from her man anymore, the anxiety hooked up with her next high-risk activity, flying in an airplane. She began to avoid flying, and the fear grew into a full-blown phobia.

♦ *Body dysphoria (the feeling that some part of your body is offensive and unacceptable)*

So many women in the past few years have complained that a certain part of their bodies is offensive and absolutely unacceptable. A recent article in *The New York Times* discussed the prevalence of this problem. More and more people, men and women alike, are receiving the diagnosis of body dysphoria. They believe, for example, that their nose is terribly ugly or that their thighs are abhorent. Even though their belief is often unrealistic and defies the consensus of others, they have developed a fixed idea about the feature in question. We see this problem in many approval cravers. In an attempt to understand why they may not be getting the level of attention and approval they believe they need, they latch onto this explanation: some part of their face or body is so ugly that everybody sees it and is offended. Therefore, approval and love from others is impossible.

Lonnie, a twenty-three-year-old acting student, was constantly enraged over the fact that she had not gotten her big break on the New York stage or the Hollywood screen. She considered herself talented and reasonably attractive and could not understand why she had not yet been discovered. As time progressed, she developed an obsession about her nose, even though to my eye and the friends and acquaintances she queried, her nose was fine for her face. Lonnie visited five plastic surgeons, reviewing over and over what they would do to improve her looks. Lonnie was actually seeking a reason to explain why she had not become a star.

◆ *Eating disorders*

Anorexia nervosa, bulimia, and other eating disorders have been demonstrated to be highly related to approval craving. These conditions particularly develop in families who set very high standards for their children, particularly the female children. The children are taught that approval, acknowledgment, and even love are always conditional, and are dependent on how they look and what image they present to the world, particularly how thin they are and how well they match the traditional Barbie doll notion of American beauty.

Bonnie, a twenty-year-old suffering from bulimia for the past few years, came from such a family. They were devastatingly critical and terribly image-conscious. Everything had to be the best: the country club, the silverware, the car, the clothes. The family's entire focus was trained on impressing others. The mother had kept herself at 107 pounds for the last fifteen years through starvations, spas, and rabid and excessive exercise.

◆ *Hypchondriasis (overconcern with one's health)*

We see hypochondriasis in many unassertive individuals—those who cannot express their feelings authentically and directly to others or who cannot stand up for their rights and are afraid of negative evaluation. In an interesting twist, they often come to focus a good deal of negative attention on their bodies, feeling more and more vulnerable as the weeks, months, and years pass. They visit doctors frequently, complaining of imagined ills. They feel good only if a doctor tells them that, yes, they do have something wrong and prescribes a pill. Every ache and pain becomes a major calamity. It's as if these people simply don't feel a sense of mastery or control over their lives. They feel bullied by the world, taken advantage of. They don't have the skills to assert themselves, so they seem to turn on themselves with the belief that their body is always failing them, is extremely vulnerable.

Roberta, a twenty-seven-year-old design trainee at a large fashion house in New York, came to see me with two major problems. One, she was a severe approval craver, particularly with her boyfriend, from whom she accepted a good deal of abuse and exploitation, and two, she was a patient who had what I call "the complaint of the week" syndrome. Roberta spent nearly all of her salary on doctors' bills, even though she was reassured week after week about the various complaints she presented to various doctors. Her genuine, legitimate complaints such as sore throats and strained muscles were greatly magnified into "incurable illnesses." As we worked on Roberta's approval craving and got her to challenge her need to have her boyfriend and others in her life love and approve of her all the time, and as she came to recognize that she could live happily without that constant love and approval, her hypochondriasis dropped away. Roberta's case was one of the more dramatic instances in which someone who was filled with somatic complaints improved almost miraculously, once she took control of her approval craving.

♦ *Various stress symptoms that manifest in physical symptomology (headaches, colitis, stomach aches, hyperventilation, ulcers, nervous tics, and so on)*

With these patients, we always look for unresolved or unspoken conflicts and pain about lack of approval. Charlene, a thirty-one-year-old who was happy in many aspects of her life, complained of tension headaches. Upon probing, we discovered that any time her boyfriend disapproved of her, she couldn't defend herself. She would fall apart and then work double time to win back his approval. This would nearly always precipitate a tension headache, yet Charlene had never made the connection because he often would not vocally disapprove of her; she would simply believe or anticipate that he would disapprove. Once she made the connection, learned skills to reduce her tension, and learned to value herself without her boyfriend's blessing of everything she did, Charlene's headaches faded.

As we complete our overview of the symptoms and situations associated with approval craving, see if some of the following styles and characteristics are familiar to you.

### ♦ "I'm Nothing Without You"

The approval craver has the absolute belief that she will perish without her partner's approval and constant reassurance. Whenever they believe that approval is not forthcoming, these people are ruled by very powerful and influential self-images that they are almost invisible or lacking in any substance and value.

Peggy, an attractive twenty-six-year-old, would date many men, but would report that whenever she sat down to dinner, she felt almost invisible—very, very little in the big chair at dinner. As her date paid her more attention, complimented her, made her laugh—made her feel the center of his world—she would feel herself grow in the chair, developing more and more mass. When he failed to do that, either by design or simply because he was distracted by something else, Peggy would sink back into the feeling of being tiny or nearly invisible in the chair.

### ♦ The Fatal Attraction

This person will do anything to hold onto her partner because she cannot tolerate his being interested in another woman. When a woman I had dated before I married discovered my serious interest in the woman I did marry, she began leaving anonymous notes on my car, making all sorts of cruel fabrications about my fiancée. Two or three years after I married, I ran into this woman in the street, and we decided to have coffee. I confronted her with what she had done. She owned up to her acts, and told me she had felt so insecure and desperate to hold onto the relationship with me, and so angry that I was interested in someone else, that, yes, she had posted a number of those ugly, anonymous notes that purported to warn me of the danger I was in.

### ♦ Little Miss Innocent

This person is truly naive and innocent. She really believes that by being totally compliant she'll earn his undying love, protection, and attention forever. This person often ends up with a sociopath or con man.

Inez, a twenty-year-old waitress, grew up in a household in which the mother was extremely compliant toward the father. Whereas the father was not cruel, he was certainly controlling and somewhat bullying of the mother, Inez, and two other sisters. Inez observed how her mother would calm her husband down by cooking his favorite meals, actually bathing him at times, wearing his favorite outfits, and other placating behaviors. On at least three occasions, Inez used this total subservient behavior to win men's interest and keep them in a relationship. But she attracted manipulative, con-men types who could instinctively sniff out her willingness to be exploited. Inez would place bets for these men and loan them money, and, in one case, she actually shoplifted for a man in order to win his approval.

♦ *The Great Imposter*

This individual has convinced herself that she's reached whatever position she has in life by fooling people. One day she will be found out to be ignorant, uneducated, of poor judgment, and basically a fool. She runs around and around, constantly trying to win approval from others to bolster her flagging ego, to buy insurance for another day that she won't be found out as the inadequate person she believes she really is.

Daphne, a thirty-eight-year-old public relations executive, was absolutely convinced that she had fooled everybody and achieved her position simply because she is good at conning people. Someday, Daphne was certain, her entire charade would collapse on her. The reality was that she was a well-educated, bright, gregarious person, but Daphne had suffered excessive criticism from her parents and older brother and had become convinced that she was stupid and whatever she attempted was guaranteed to fail. Her older brother had even labeled her "the jinx," and in high school, a few teachers had mocked her in class, so Daphne had developed a poor image of herself. Daphne's daydreams were filled with images of being found out by her boss and colleagues, and she was reluctant to speak publicly for fear of seeming an inadequate fool, despite overwhelming evidence of her competence and the respect she elicited from others on the job and in social situations. Even with her boyfriend, she would prepare for their dates by boning up on current events, on reviews of movies they would see, just so she would have all the right things to say and would not be found out as an imposter.

♦ *Turn the Other Cheek*

Women who are abused regularly, emotionally or physically, by a boyfriend who humiliates them in public and is insanely jealous and emotionally ungenerous, often offer no defense. They are so hooked on the occasional times when he is attentive and loving that they block or numb the pain. Battered women often manifest this syndrome.

Twenty-five-year-old model Deidre was psychologically and emotionally battered. If she even looked at another man, her boyfriend would fly into a jealous rage, but Deidre would just stand there and offfer no defense at all. When I asked why she did not point out to him how inappropriate his childish behavior was and why she was so passive, she would offer in his defense his frequently loving nature. She didn't see a reason to respond to his outbursts and also mentioned that she was shell-shocked by his jealous rages and that any confrontation she might offer would not get through. I asked if she ever walked out of the room, but Deidre said she was afraid he would lock her out. Like many others who turn the other cheek, Deidre would also act in a passive-aggressive manner. That is, she would stay out late, even when her boyfriend expected her home, so that she could indirectly express her anger and punish him. Only after therapy was Deidre able to directly confront him.

♦ *"Men are Gods"*

These women will only listen to the opinions of men. They will only act decisively when a man gives his blessing to the behavior or activity.

Sandra owned her own jewelry company, but it was primarily a male-dominated industry. Even though she was considered an innovator within the industry, she would not make a move concerning money, purchases, or sales, without checking first with a network of men she had established within the industry with whom she could consult. All indications were that Sandra's own judgments were perfectly fine. She had built and ran a very successful company, but she was convinced almost superstitiously that she could not act effectively and successfully without a man's blessing, or at least his opinion.

### ◆ *Blind Loyalties*

No matter how unhappy they are, these women feel they must stick with their man. We discussed many of these women in our previous book, *Bailing Out: The Healthy Way to Get Out of a Bad Relationship and Survive*. They deny the pain they feel or even if they don't deny it, somehow they believe it's the right or moral or obligatory behavior to stick with their man. They constantly hope against hope that he will change. We see these women as enablers of alcoholics and other addicts. They are frequently found in co-dependent Twelve Step programs, such as Al-Anon. These loyalists constantly struggle to learn how to not enable and how to know they can live without a man in their lives and still be happy and effective.

Forty-two-year-old Doreen had been involved for a number of years with a fifty-year-old husband who had been an alcoholic and was in recovery. Although he was in AA, the man still engaged in a number of harmful and humiliating behaviors with Doreen, in particular, attacking her for poor parenting skills. More than once Doreen had consulted psychologists and attorneys about leaving the relationship. In fact, Doreen was one of the chief inspirations for this second book. Part of Doreen's problem was solved by the steps taught in *Bailing Out*, but she also had to recognize for the future how to overcome the blind loyalty that she had learned from her mother who had supported her alcoholic husband no matter what. After therapy, Doreen was able to challenge her distorted ideas concerning what she owed her partner.

# CHAPTER 2

# ASSESSING THE ORIGINS OF YOUR APPROVAL CRAVING

♦

This chapter will help you identify the important incidents and developmental milestones in your life that have led to the formation of certain crippling life rules. It is axiomatic that if you don't get approval in childhood or you are punished inordinately, you will crave approval as an adult. Early messages and rules formed in childhood such as "I must do all that I can in order to get my parents to love me," or "Being wrong or making a mistake will be terribly humiliating," are the emotional foundation that determines the conscious or nonconscious need to win complete approval within a love relationship.

This chapter will help you discover your own rules about punishment and praise by helping you answer the following question: What messages did I get early in life that taught me to base my self-worth on what others think of me?

Nina, a twenty-six-year-old stockbroker trainee, complained about her boyfriend's reluctance to spend time with her family. He only wanted to spend time with his own. When she asked him why, he answered that they appeared very self-involved, emotionally withholding, and selfish. After Nina thought the matter over, she realized that one of the primary messages she had received from her family as a child was that she could only be valued as a person if she pleased them, if she performed for them. This sense of early contingent acceptance is surprisingly common, and it leaves its mark in our adult lives. As an adult, Nina was extremely dependent on her boyfriend's approval, spending most of her time thinking about how to please him and how she might have alienated him. Her efforts came not from love and concern, but from a sense of impending doom, that any moment she would commit that fatal error and her boyfriend would judge her harshly and break up with her. Like so many of us, Nina had learned to define her self-worth by others' approval of not only her person but her actions.

What is the importance of discovering exactly what are the early messages fueling your own approval craving? The first reason is that you will be more cooperative in your own self-therapy if you know how these pieces came together. Insight is important because it makes you more willing to work on the various exercises in this book and to stay motivated when the going gets tough. Another reason for learning your own life messages is that you will be clearer about where to assign the responsiblity for your approval craving.

If you become aware of some of the messages you learned as a child, you will be able to depersonalize the blame, to shift responsiblity away from yourself to some degree and toward the source of your problem: your parents or others who either gave you early messages or behaved in a way that instigated the beginnings of your approval craving. Once you acquire a full appreciation of the many years of reinforcement—particularly during the vulnerable stage of childhood—that allowed these beliefs and the extraordinary need for approval to develop, you will begin to understand why your approval craving is so difficult to overcome.

Pamela, a thirty-six-year-old bank teller, craved approval from her customers, her boss, her co-workers, and, most importantly, from the men in her life. Typically she spent an inordinate amount of time worrying if she was doing the right thing, if she was dressing appropriately, and if she struck others as uncouth. When I suggested to her that it was important for her to review her background, she protested. "But you're a behavior therapist," she said. "I came to you to work on behavioral changes, on current, present issues, not on past issues." I pointed out to Pamela that it was essential to focus on these issues for the reasons just described. Pamela resisted delving into her past; she only wanted to role play, to do other exercises, and to change her belief systems. Therapy failed miserably. When we finally went back to the drawing board to review her past, Pamela acquired an understanding as to how all of the pieces of her life came together into her approval-craving pattern. From that point on, her therapy progressed swiftly.

As a behavior therapist, I generally do not spend a good deal of time on a patient's history, but such an exploration leading to an understanding of how she developed approval-craving behaviors is necessary in order to overcome this pervasive problem.

Parents are supposed to love us without our having to work for that love. Most people who report approval craving as an adult have a history of either receiving inconsistent love or feeling that other siblings were favored; have addicted, emotionally troubled parents; have an absent parent; or have overly critical parents. Somehow they felt they had to struggle mightily to achieve the right formula to win love, or that love may not have even been available to them.

If you did not receive the security of that unconditional love, you could spend your life struggling for the formula that will finally bring you what you have missed for so long. To interrupt that futile struggle, you must know exactly what happened to you. You must understand why you struggled for love and approval from an early age.

Throughout childhood, our parents teach us which of our behaviors are acceptable and not acceptable by hugging, praising, and punishing. The frequency and intensity of self-effacing thoughts and behaviors, and, consequently, the level of our approval craving as adults, is directly related to these early punishing events. There are at least five factors related to parental punishment that determine the negative impact on self-esteem and disapproval fear that you experience today.

1. The frequency of punitive measures. The frequency of negative messages from parents and significant others has a profound impact on childhood feelings of worth and well-being. Occasional punitive messages are far less damaging than unremitting and highly frequent punishing messages.

2. The consistency of punitive messages. If parents are consistent in telling the child they don't like cursing or other inappropriate behavior, the child learns this as wrong behavior and drops the behavior. If, however, parenting is inconsistent, the child will feel guilt. The child is certain he has done wrong but can never get the rule straight. Having no idea of what he has done wrong, he blames himself.

3. The degree to which parents are unable to distinguish between punishing the *behavior* of the child and punishing the *selfhood* of the child. If a child hears "You're a bad boy" over and over again when the parent is trying to punish a particular behavior, the child's ability to distinguish between badness and bad behavior becomes blurred. He doesn't learn the difference between what he's *done* and what he *is*. Such children grow into adulthood feeling that any transgression or mistake they make will increase their own core of badness and cause others to feel badly about them. Therefore, they will do whatever they can to garner approval at any cost.

4. Whether or not parents describe issues of taste or good judgment as moral imperatives. A child is often made to feel morally wrong if mother wants him to cut his hair and he refuses, or if he risks injury by skiing, against mother's wishes. The parent doesn't view the activity as poor judgment but as something truly bad. The child is "lazy" or "selfish" or "looks like a homeless person" or is "nutty."

5. The frequency with which punishing messages are tied to anger or rejection. Children can usually handle a reasonable level of criticism without becoming overly hurt or maligned. But if the criticism is constantly associated with intense parental anger or withdrawal of love and caring (either threatened or actual), it can engrave a strong impression on the child, establishing a powerful image of "wrongness" that is carried into adulthood, and, of course, creating approval craving.

## Special Cases

Children from a broken home, for example, will always be troubled by the question, "If they can stop loving each other, will they stop loving me?" Another common pattern is for children to observe contingent love between parents. One parent seems to crave approval constantly from the other, who, in turn, dispenses love erratically to his or her partner. The observing child learns that this is the normal state of affairs and begins to model that behavior.

A somewhat ironic pattern involves the overly approving parent. The child is trained to view receiving continuous approval as the norm. The parents are so concerned about denying their child approval that they constantly pay attention, use hyperbole to compliment the child, and are overprotective. The child begins to recognize early on that it's all an act—that the parents' approval is insincere—and comes to distrust most of what the parents say. That particular childhood pattern creates an adult who is either mistrustful of any approval they receive or who craves in every relationship of their adult life the extremely high level of approval they became accustomed to as a child. Everyone is compared to that overly attentive parent.

Gladys, a seventy-two-year-old grandmother, recalls her mother assuring her when she complained of a pimple: "Leave it alone! It's beautiful!" Everything Gladys did, according to her mother, was perfect and wonderful. Gladys felt she had never received enough constructive criticism. When she became a mother herself, she deliberately withheld all compliments from her own daughter and treated her instead to a steady barrage of corrective advice, justifying her own hypercritical behavior as true concern.

## Exploring Your Past Without a Therapist

You can identify the nature of your childhood experiences and how these experiences shaped the important messages you received, and the approval craving that plagues you today, by using various techniques.

♦ *Visualization Exercise*

Using fantasy and imagery, take us, the writers of the book, on a walk through your childhood. Take us on a tour of your past, through the rooms of your neighborhood, your childhood home, and into the living room where you discussed matters with your parents. Be as detailed as you can. This tour will trigger memories that have been long dormant but are still inscribed in your consciousness, asserting some influence on your present life, even if that influence is no longer direct and functional. The goal is to recall how you received approval, love, and affection as a child.

Use a tape recorder to describe what you see and to preserve your impressions as you make this journey. Turn the tape recorder on, then lie or sit back and close your eyes.

Take us through each room of your house. Start with the kitchen, which is often the family gathering place. What are the sounds you hear? What is the layout of the kitchen? Where are the appliances? Where do you usually sit? Recall a particular meal with the family. Who's talking? What are they saying? How are you interacting with your siblings? Are any relatives or friends present? What is the discussion about? What are the smells of the food? Is there a sense of homeyness? Is everyone involved in mealtime preparation, in cooking?

Move on to your bedroom. What does it look like? How is it decorated? Where is the bed? Is there a bulletin board? Who else is also there interacting with you? What is the first thing you see when you awake and the last thing you see when you fall asleep?

Where is your school homework done? Can you recall any pleasant memories in your room, chatting with friends? Playing with a sibling? Having a long, caring, intimate talk with a parent about your problems? Do you have such intimate discussions in your bedroom, or do you feel lonely and sad or imprisoned there?

Go through other rooms of the house: living room, den or parlor, basement, parents' bedroom. How is each laid out? What distinct memories emerge as you, a child, take us on this tour of your house? If there was more than one childhood house, does one stand out as a place where distinctive, important things occurred? Do you remember bringing things home for your parents to look at? In what room would that take place?

Go outside. Is there a backyard or a porch? What happens there? Focus primarily on interactions with parents, siblings, and peers.

Explore the neighborhood. Do you play ball on an athletic field or other games in a playground with other children? What is the interaction like? Do you go to other children's homes? Do you feel lonely, sad, and detached, or connected and accepted within the neighborhood?

Laying out precisely the physical surroundings of your childhood home is important because it creates a living context for memories to be awakened and flow into your present consciousness.

After you've completed the tour, you will have the recorded experience to process. Listen to your journey, think about it, try to understand it, and try to connect that early experience to adult experiences—that is, make sense out of these childhood memories.

Use the following questions as a guide toward uncovering your early experiences with approval and rejection. The key here is whether or not your experiences were explained to you in a manner you could understand clearly, so that you didn't personalize everything, so that you knew your failures were not entirely of your own doing.

- What was it like when you brought home school grades to your parents? How did they respond?
- How did they respond when you shared an accomplishment with them in math, in gym, or other school or neighborhood

activities? When you were excited and elated, how did they respond?

- How did they respond when you came home with a poor grade or when you failed to accomplish a goal?
- How did they respond when you did something adventurous, or self-assertive, or a bit risky?
- How did they respond when you came home feeling rejected by other children?
- How did they respond if you performed a household chore imperfectly?
- How did they respond toward your adolescent struggles for independence? The first time you wanted to wear makeup, to go out alone with friends, to go on a date, to drive the family car?
- How did they respond to your squabbles with your siblings? Did they seem to favor a brother or sister over you?
- How did they respond when you asserted yourself? For example, if you came home and complained about a teacher?
- How did they respond when you confided problems to your parents? For example, if you weren't invited to a party, or felt you were the shortest (or tallest, thinnest, fattest, or least popular) kid in the class, what was their reaction?

How did your parents explain these experiences to you? Were they accepting of you even when you failed or were less than ideal? Did your parents explain your failures in such a way that you were able to retain your self-confidence and move on?

Dr. Lubetkin recalls not being chosen a few times when the boys were picking baseball teams. He went home feeling glum and told his parents. Fortunately, they were wise enough to counsel him. They explained that people choose their teams for a number of reasons other than the ability to play ball. They choose their friends first, and it wasn't that important that Barry be the number one choice. As long as *he* knew he was a good baseball player, that was all that mattered. Dr. Lubetkin would come away from these talks feeling understood, and that was all that really mattered.

Dr. Oumano, on the other hand, recalls receiving a D grade in a math class for her last semester of high school. She had already been accepted to the college of her choice, so in the time-honored tradition of high school seniors, she passed her last semester having fun rather than studying. The report cards were given out during graduation exercises, and Dr. Oumano still remembers her parents' anger and disappointment and how her own feeling of failure dampened what should have been a happy occasion.

Kathleen, a forty-eight-year-old writer, still remembers the humiliation of being teased as a young adolescent every morning at the bus stop by a neighbor. Her parents never sat down to talk the matter over with her. But the boy's mother invited Kathleen in for milk and cookies, assured the girl that this was normal behavior for boys, and told her that in a few years they would be asking her for a date. Kathleen left the woman's home feeling much better about herself and confident of her future glamour.

If the adult explanation includes such truisms as "Rejection happens to everyone," "It could be the other person's problem," "They could secretly like you but they just don't know how to express it," "No one is liked by everyone," or "Anyone who makes superficial negative judgments about you isn't worth liking," whether or not these truths apply, the explanation helps the child feel better about herself and more self-accepting.

If you did not receive the consolation such explanations provide, you are likely to have personalized and internalized these "failure" experiences, to have read them as a sign that you are severely lacking. You will not be able to accept or approve of yourself and will therefore seek approval from others to compensate. You will also do anything to avoid rejection.

♦ *Visualize your interactions with your siblings.*

Were you in the shadow of a sibling? Younger siblings are often less neuroticized by their parents. The parents are less protective and are more encouraging of adventuresome behavior and risk-taking. Younger children are often more extroverted, less inhibited, and often put the older children in the shadows. The older siblings tend to be overprotected and more shy. Many of my patients who are older children visualize themselves playing with their siblings and feeling overshadowed by the younger ones. This is particularly true of middle children, who report feeling lost. If you are a middle child, visualize what demands were made of you within the home. For example, middle children are often told to take responsiblity for the younger kids, but they don't receive reinforcement from the parents for this task. Older children receive reinforcement, and younger children receive attention for being cute, but the middle children don't reap any of this positive attention.

Dr. Oumano, the oldest of three, feels she received the brunt of negative attention and criticism and was told she had to put up with the antics of her younger brothers because she was the oldest. Her younger brother, the middle boy, feels his older sister received all of the attention and that his younger brother was considered cuter. Her youngest brother feels he was dismissed as a cute little idiot.

♦ *How was the birth of a sibling explained to you?*

Bonnie was six years old when her baby brother was born. She wasn't told a new baby was on the way, except in the vaguest of terms. About a week before the new baby was due, she was shipped off to an uncle and aunt for five weeks. When she returned home, there was the new baby, *in her place*! Bonnie felt tremendous resentment toward him, and for years described strong homicidal urges toward her brother. Bonnie had felt she was rejected for something terribly wrong she must have done when she was sent away and replaced with this new intruder. As an adult, Bonnie was overconcerned with her image. She had to behave perfectly at work and socially; she was always up on the latest fashions, drove the latest model prestige car, and was generally overly concerned about the impression she projected.

♦ *Interview family members, particularly parents and siblings.*

Interviewing your parents about your childhood is an unusual tool, but it can prove to be surprisingly effective. Parents often block out events, and they tend to become defensive. We feel embarrassed and uncomfortable about questioning our parents about events that happened to us in the past. But the point is that for many of you, your parents will make themselves accessible if you present this as a project for your own self-understanding and that there is no better way of digging up the evidence, of finding out what happened, than by going to the source.

Prepare your parents. Explain that you're working on problems of shyness and unassertiveness, of worrying about what others think of you, and of image-making, and you could use their help in working through these problems. Explain that your goal is not to blame them; you simply would be a much happier person if you could understand these past issues.

The following is a list of possible questions you could direct to your parents.

- How was I reinforced and complimented for my accomplishments?
- When I craved attention as a child, either from you or from other adults, how was that handled?
- How was sibling rivalry resolved?
- How was rejection explained to me? (Rejection includes being teased or left out.)
- If there was a separation or divorce, how was that explained to me?
- What explanation did I receive about the birth of a new baby?
- When I was frustrated or disappointed, how was I comforted?
- Was I encouraged to be reasonably adventurous?
- Was I taught to be a risk-taker and who was the risk-taker in the family who served as my model?
- When I idolized somebody, how was that explained to me? How was I helped to understand why I was idolizing others?
- Was I as a person condemned or was my behavior criticized? In other words, how did you criticize me? What were the types of things you said to me? Was I told my *behavior* was bad or that I was a bad girl?
- Was I ever told I was good the way I am? How was I told that I was good just the way I was? Or was my goodness always contingent upon doing something well, on my behavior and accomplishments?

- How consistent were you in punishing me for misbehavior, or was it random?

Add your own questions. These exercises are not designed to give you definitive answers as much as to start you on the process of gaining insight into how your approval-craving patterns developed. Once you have imagined these various situations and how you and your parents handled them, keep the record of these memories in order to refer to them periodically as you proceed through this book. Simply thinking about what you have retrieved and recorded from memory will automatically clear certain issues and explain much of your behavior.

Many clients report insights such as, "Of course I keep running after men for approval. I never received it from my dad." We call these insights the "aha" phenomenon, where suddenly the light bulb turns on and you understand, perhaps for the first time, the connection between present behavior and a pattern that began in childhood. That's all this work is about—making connections.

Look over your parents' answers. Were they straightforward and honest in their responses, or were they circumspect and unable or unwilling to give you any real information?

### ♦ *Incomplete Sentences*

Ask your parents and/or siblings to complete the following sentences. Then fill in the blanks for the questions that seem appropriate to answer yourself. This technique is a nonthreatening way to get our parents and ourselves to take a more objective look at our childhood.

- When my child (I) was young, to get attention, she (I) would
  _____ .

- The first time I knew my child (I) was insecure was when _____ .
- I couldn't stand it when my child (I) would _____ .
- I wished that my child (I) would have been more confident about _____ .
- I wish my child (I) would have been more _____ .
- I wish my child (I) would have been less _____ .

- My child (I) seemed most humiliated and embarrassed when
  _____ .
- My child (I) would get so hurt by _____ .
- My child (I) disappointed me (myself) when _____ .
- My child (I) made me (myself) proud when _____ .
- My child (I) made me (myself) angry when _____ .
- The way I failed my child most as a parent was _____ .
- I could never understand why my child (I) was so sensitive
  about _____ .
- If a good friend hurt my child (me), she (I) would _____ .
- The time my child seemed (I felt) most lost and confused was
  _____ .
- My child (I) idolized _____ .
- If my child received a bad school grade, I would
  say _____ .
- If my child was rejected by friends, I would _____ .

Again, the point of this exercise is to find clues about how your
approval craving and fear of rejection began and why you're defining your worth today based on what other people think of you.

## Reviewing Recent Life Experiences

Let's see how recent life experiences have reinforced your approval
craving and rejection anxiety, and compare your current thoughts
and behaviors to those you've been able to reconstruct from the
past. Let's examine key areas of your life.

### ♦ Work

If your boss's approval is somewhat inconsistent—that is,
similar to your childhood home life—you will most likely respond
to his waxing and waning approval in a manner that matches your
childish reaction to your parents' seemingly inconsistent love.
Even though your childhood experiences and how they were dealt
with gave birth to your approval craving, it is the reinforcement and strengthening these beliefs receive throughout your life
that turns them into persistent habits. Someone with an inconsis-

tent parent who was lucky enough to work his first several jobs with an attentive, supportive supervisor will be less needy of approval than if he worked for inconsistent, nonsupportive bosses. On the other hand, if such a person does eventually work for a difficult person who inconsistently dispenses approval, that situation might push a forgotten button, and approval-craving behavior might result.

Florence, a fifty-year-old professor, had enjoyed working at a small New England college. When her husband's work forced them to relocate, Florence found herself at a new university, working under a department chairman who was cold and judgmental. She found herself working overtime to avoid his disapproval and to please him. Whenever she anticipated being called into his office, she found herself perspiring and even shaking in anticipated fear. She was convinced he would reject her. After some therapy, Florence realized her chairman's behavior matched almost exactly that of her own father. Her father was distant, hypercritical, scornful, and would occasionally be warm and giving, but unpredictably would withdraw into his critical and judgmental mode. Once Florence understood what buttons were being pushed, she was able to handle her work situation much more easily.

Another example is Stephanie, a music business publicist, who was troubled by a backstabbing colleague. The colleague constantly bad-mouthed her, but what troubled Stephanie more was her own overreaction. She would go home, cry, and feel completely unworthy. She couldn't understand why she was overreacting this way. After completing some of the previous exercises, Stephanie realized this current experience paralleled an old sibling rivalry with her older sister. Stephanie believed the sister had been favored by her parents and always seemed to get better presents and cuter dates. Stephanie would take it out on her sister by tearing out a page of her diary or ripping a favorite blouse. Whether Stephanie's perceptions were real or not was irrelevant in terms of therapy. Once Stephanie realized that she was essentially reenacting that same conflict with her sister and that those experiences had no relation to her present life, she was much better able to handle her difficult colleague. She was no longer passive-aggressive, as she had been with her sister, but more assertive, straightforward, and calm.

♦ *Relationships*

Similar generalizations can be made about women who continually find themselves involved with mysterious, withholding men. They feel intimidated by these men, fear any form of rejection, and continually search for ways to win their approval. The men continue to be inconsistent in terms of their loving and to value the woman only in terms of how the woman makes them feel. If you are such a woman, you probably learned in childhood that love is equated somehow with withholding. Your parents were withholding, and you constantly sought the right formula to make your parents consistently loving, attentive, and nurturing. Early on, you learned the blueprint that love equals withholding, so you seek out men who are withholding because that is your understanding of the nature of love and intimacy.

# Habitual Beliefs and Behaviors
# Learned in Special Situations

♦ *The Abusive and Alcoholic Family: "I can't trust."*

Abusive and alcoholic family patterns are quite similar. The single most important element is the lack of trust and inconsistency that develops. Chaos reigns wherever there is an alcoholic and abusive parent. The child never knows when the parent will be loving or drunk and abusive, and seeks in vain for the right formula to control the parent's behavior. The child is stuck trying to make sense from nonsense.

The other element commonly found in the alcoholic or otherwise abusive household is unpredictable anger. Everyone in the family is kept on edge; when is the drunk going to blow up? Often the child becomes a pawn between the parents, trying to ameliorate disputes and head off disaster. Approval craving and fear of rejection become of paramount concern to the child.

Sylvia grew up with a very unpredictable father. When he was not drinking, he was a warm, loving individual who gave her gifts and called her his little princess. She remembers hours spent snuggled on his lap with him being loving and attentive. But about once a week he would spend the night drinking with his friends, and when he returned home, he would be full of rage—cursing, violent toward the mother, throwing objects about, and yelling he was sorry he ever saddled himself with a wife and family. He would be better off on his own or even dead, he'd rage. Believing every word he said, the children would run to a far corner of a back room, cowering in fear. They learned behaviors to predict their father's behavior. One child would act as scout, peering out the window. If he saw the father being driven home, they knew he was drunk, and they would all try to hide. If it was payday, they knew he would get drunk, so they would all make play dates and try to be absent from the house. They would even try to be extra nice to their father when he was in a drunken rage, pleading with him, and attempting to make peace between him and their mother. Their lives revolved around anticipating how this man would behave and trying to soften his behavior. As adults, Sylvia and her siblings continued this pattern. Although Sylvia couldn't understand why her mother stayed with this man, she also remembered very positive experiences with her father, and that was the source of her confusion. That's why she and her brother lacked trust and feared unpredictability. They had never developed a consistent belief set about the drunken parent.

♦ *The Broken Home: "Love is temporary. When it goes, I'm to blame because I'm unlovable."*

Children from a broken home commonly believe that the parents have fallen out of love or that one has left the home "because of me." They believe their one-parent household is a unique situation. They feel that love from the parent who left was never really there, and so the pattern of craving love and approval begins. If there hasn't been a solid explanation for the separation that removes the blame from the child's shoulders, he will believe he is at fault. He did or even thought something that led to the parents' split. If those beliefs are not corrected, approval craving and rejection anxiety will certainly become a serious lifelong problem.

Gina's parents split up when she was nine years old. She received little explanation. Her father simply did not return home one night. Her mother received a call from him approximately one month later, and when Gina begged to be put on the phone to her father, her mother refused, saying, "I'm never going to let you talk to this animal again." The mother was trying to protect her child and punish her husband at the same time, but she never even gave Gina the opportunity to say goodbye and get any explanation. Now, as an adult, whenever Gina is dating someone, she finds herself flooded by fears of abandonment. Any clue at all that the man will possibly reject her, or is critical of her, sends her into a panic, almost an emotional paralysis. She is extremely compliant, will lie about herself to seem more appealing, and will tell the man she hasn't gone out with girlfriends if she suspects he would disapprove of that behavior. Gina completely has negated herself and her needs in order to avoid reliving that abandonment. She lives in a manner focused on avoiding a replay of that primal abandonment.

♦ *The Rigidly Moralistic and Inconsistent Home: "I must be absolutely perfect in thought and behavior to merit love. If I'm not all good, I don't deserve love."*

Black-and-white thinking reigns in these homes, which are often places of extreme religious orthodoxy. The world is viewed through inflexible moral values: things are either good or bad.

Cynthia, a thirty-two-year-old visiting nurse, was raised in such a home with a puritanical mother and a rigid, tyrannical father. Every aspect of her life was governed strictly: when she did her homework, which friends she could play with, what clothes she could wear. She was cautioned not to be sexual in any way with boys, even in high school and college. As an adult, she reported having felt as if she was imprisoned in a nunnery for years and years. The mother was an avid church-goer who would come home and read the Bible to Cynthia and insist she attend church frequently herself. Cynthia developed obsessive quirks and worries because she was always trying to ensure approval by living a moral and straight life. Cynthia was imperfect, as are all human beings, and strayed from the impossible standards set for her by her parents. She would then experience tremendous anxiety and guilt, which manifested in her relationships as an adult. She was extremely obsessive about anything sexual. If a man made an innocent overture to her, she would immediately interpret it as the man wanting to take her to bed. On one hand, she wanted to go further, but her early conditioning forced her to hold back. She came into therapy complaining of these conflicts. She was still an untouched virgin, and yet was craving love and approval. She didn't know the formula to be loose and relaxed and how to be a fun date. We did a lot of work getting her to recognize the connection of her inhibitions to her upbringing, and that she no longer lived under her parents' thumb.

♦ *The Home with an Overly Critical Parent: "I must be perfect to be loved."*

This home is similar to the one previous, but the point in this home is that the parent is perfectionistic about the child. They make extraordinary demands on the child in terms of school work, comportment, and express extreme disappointment and anger if the child deviates from this high standard of behavior. The child becomes terrified of risk-taking, because he might earn the parent's disapproval. The child also feels resentment, even hate, because peer pressure to break these rules, to be playful, is powerful. So the child feels torn between peer pressure and the expectations of the parents. These people often have serious emotional breakdowns or become drug or alcohol abusers. When they do finally rebel, if they can rebel, they do so with a vengeance.

Raylene, a thirty-five-year-old artist, was raised by a perfectionistic mother. Rather than kowtow to her mother's impossible demands, Raylene rebelled from an early age. Her entire childhood, particularly her adolescence, was a struggle of wills between herself and her mother. Raylene rebelled but, deep down, she had internalized what she felt was her mother's message of disapproval. In order to break free of her mother's stifling strictures, Raylene developed a pattern of universal rebellion—whether or not it was justified by the situation—that masked her own self-rejection.

This rebellious attitude and behavior became a way of life, along with an extreme fear of anticipated criticism and a pattern of inappropriate and self-destructive behaviors.

♦ *The Home in Which a Parent Was Fearful or Passive: "If they're afraid of it, then it must be dangerous."*

If the parent is passive, fearful, or socially inept and unable to take risks, the child lacks a model for healthy, assertive behavior. The child receives an incomplete education about how to get what she wants in life, and learns instead to anticipate failure and rejection, as did her parent. These people come to therapy with mastery complaints. They suffer a "crisis of the week" and are unable to assert themselves and gain the approval they desire. Often these people will seek out a strong, authoritative partner to guide them and teach them the rules of living. If they are lucky, they find such a helpful person. If they're unlucky, they find an exploiter who recognizes their lost, wounded state and takes advantage of them.

Rene, a twenty-nine-year-old executive secretary, came to therapy each week complaining of one or another crises in living. Usually, these crises involved some naivete or innocence on her part about basic social rules and skills. For example, we spent most of one session on explanations of the amounts for tips Rene should give to the various workers in her cooperative apartment building—information that is readily available from friends, articles, and general life experience. Yet Rene continued to seek out authoritative life guidance with even the most minor of life's rules. Rene would also manifest this behavior in relationships with boyfriends. She would appear innocent and vulnerable, tapping into their protective instincts, but, after a while, it became so chronic that they would either grow irritated or exploit her naiveté in one way or another.

In order for people to change and improve their lives, they must modify unhelpful, destructive thought patterns and behavioral patterns. However, one of the greatest reasons why people resist change in my form of active therapy is because they are missing any insight or understanding as to how the problems originally evolved. Many people will stubbornly resist making changes in their lives until they have a fuller understanding of how to put the pieces of the puzzle together. Other people will not change until they are able to feel in their guts the very real connections between earlier experiences in their lives and the problems they are having now. Intellectual insight for these people is simply not enough. They need to really make a feeling connection between what happened when they were young and the resistances, defenses, and fears they are experiencing as adults. This chapter has been about helping you get in touch with some of those earlier experiences by reviewing your past, by reviewing your history, and by getting a better sense as to the types of psychological processes that shaped you into an approval craver. It is much more likely that you are going to be able to move forward quickly rather than hesitantly in conquering your fear.

# CHAPTER 3

# IDENTIFYING UNHEALTHY THOUGHTS AND STYLES OF DISTORTED THINKING

♦

Approval craving is like a locomotive. In order to run, it must have fuel in the form of distorted thinking. If approval cravers take a closer look at their styles of thinking, they will discover they are victims of automatic thoughts that flash into their heads through-out their day and feed their approval craving and create their approval-seeking behavior.

To illustrate how certain beliefs you might hold represent distorted views of reality, we can examine how others might interpret the same event. For example, people seated in a restaurant might observe a mother bawling out her young child. Each person will view the incident differently, depending on their particular cognitive set, the particular way they think about things, and the particular place they are in their lives. Another mother might feel sympathetic toward the mother because she experiences similar problems with her own children. A child abuse expert might be concerned, thinking the mother overly punitive. A child sitting at the next table might feel empathetic toward the child who is being yelled at. The point is that this single situation can be experienced with a different set of feelings by different people observing the same interaction between mother and child.

Another example is the Clarence Thomas/Anita Hill sexual harrassment issue. People displayed wildly different reactions to the same information based on their varying cognitive sets. A woman who has been taught to be compliant and to capitulate to authority will be shocked at Anita Hill's public accusations toward her former boss, especially when he had recommended her highly for subsequent positions and was about to be confirmed to the Supreme Court. Professor Hill should be grateful for his help, the compliant woman might say, rather than dragging up old griev-ances. The woman who has been raised to believe that, in fact, there are men who will take advantage of women, will feel very differ-ently. She will likely side with Professor Hill, believing that Professor Hill is within her rights and behaving appropriately. A woman who has been harassed on the job and passed over for a promotion will likely feel even more empathy toward Professor Hill's concerns.

The distorted thinking that develops throughout our childhood and early adulthood is the single most common factor leading to approval craving. Cognitive therapy goes to that root factor, help-ing you to identify and correct those distorting thoughts and belief systems. The following explanation and history will help you better understand how cognitive behavior therapy can help you overcome your craving for approval.

# Cognitive Behavior Therapy and Social Learning Theory

Cognitive behavior therapy was developed in the Fifties out of basic disaffection with long-term psychoanalytic therapy. Many dissatisfied practitioners of psychotherapy felt analytic therapy took too long and was not really relevant for helping people deal with current crises in their lives.

At the same time, there was a growth in the scientific study of psychotherapy. Before this time, there had not been an interest in assessing progress in therapy and determining which specific elements in therapy were effecting positive change. People just assumed a course of psychotherapy would make them "better," but no one had ever questioned whether this belief was, in fact, true.

Once the process of behavioral change was investigated scientifically, more and more focus was placed on the importance of general learning theory. Learning theory became the theoretical bulwark of what was first known as behavior therapy. Later, when behavior therapy was expanded to what we now refer to as cognitive behavior therapy, social learning theory became the general theoretical framework with which to understand motivation for thought as well as behavior.

Social learning theory simply states that the laws of learning that have shaped our behaviors can also be used to help us extinguish nonadaptive behaviors and thoughts that do not produce positive results in our lives. One example of social learning is modeling, the learning of a behavior by observing others engaging in it. Children learn behaviors by observing their parents as models. Another such law is reinforcement. If feelings, thoughts, or behaviors are followed by positive reinforcement—that is, actions, statements, or any other expression of approval—these behaviors are learned and strengthened. If behaviors are followed by negative reinforcement—that is, actions, statements, or any other expression of disapproval—these behaviors are weakened or extinguished. These laws of learning, therefore, help us to learn behaviors and, by the same token, help us "unlearn" or extinguish unwanted behaviors.

Originally, the only problems treated by behavior therapists were phobias, addictions, and other similarly limited problems. But with new understanding of the nature of anxiety and mood disorders, and with the addition of cognitive interventions in the sixties and seventies, the entire basis of behavior therapy was broadened. Cognitive interventions involve looking at belief systems—the life rules or mythologies people live by—the same way we look at behaviors. Over the years, people develop certain cognitions or belief systems through modeling and reinforcement. That is, they learn thought patterns from models such as parents and other authority figures, and they learn these cognitions by having "the truth" of these thoughts continually confirmed through reinforcement. Eventually, these cognitions come to rule their lives. When these cognitions are correct and self-enhancing, people feel good and are happy and successful. For example, a self-enhancing cognition might be, "My worth is based on more than just my success at work or in my relationship. I am made up of numerous talents, skills, and thoughts, and my performance at my job or in my relationship is only one part of my overall worth."

When these cognitions are distorted or negative, or when they are generally incorrect—not based on accurate data—they become "self-downing" and destructive to life. For example, a negative cognition or belief might be, "My worth is almost totally contingent on how well I do at work or how much people like me." Another example would be, "My worth is contingent on a successful marriage." If you behave according to this belief, any minor setback in your relationship or at work sets off a ripple effect that infuses every aspect of your life with feelings of unworthiness and anticipations of failure that often become self-fulfilling prophesies.

As we have observed throughout this book, these types of cognitions form in various ways. The one concerning worth based on marriage may be based on early observations and conclusions drawn from the interaction of your parents or on hearing how a favored parent has revered a marriage or defined her entire worth on how successful her marriage was to your father. A sense of worth or value based on how you perform at work has a more current source. It is often based on seeing other people's successes at work and craving that type of success yourself. The important point here, however, is that to define your entire being or self by the success you have in marriage or at work, or in any other human endeavor, is to set yourself up for a dangerous downward spiral if these experiences do not work out and match the standards you have created for them. These types of overgeneralized cognitions and beliefs and self-worth are nearly always incorrect and illogical, as we will continue to point out.

You might be aware of the beliefs or cognitions that govern your behavior. More likely, however, these thoughts are "nonconscious," not part of your conscious awareness but not necessarily hidden away in some childhood dynamic. If you want to make a reasonable decision regarding your relationship and if you want to prevent repeating the same mistakes in future relationships, it is crucial that these negative and inaccurate cognitions be identified and supplanted by more accurate, positive beliefs that produce more constructive behavior patterns.

Cognitive behavior therapy helps you accomplish just that. It helps you to modify or change thoughts through making use of the same laws of learning with which behavior therapy changes behaviors. You can learn to model new cognitions or thoughts; you can learn to rehearse new cognitions. You can learn to extinguish cognitions and you can learn to reinforce cognitions, just as you can learn to model, rehearse, extinguish, and reinforce behaviors. With the addition of "cognitive" (thought) to "behavior" (action), the effectiveness of the entire therapeutic endeavor is increased.

So much human misery is unnecessary, stemming from incorrect conclusions we make about the world. Our interpretations—what we tell ourselves—create the various negative emotions that lead us to feel upset and unhappy. One person can look at another's sour face and feel rejected because he is trapped in a particular cognitive set. Another can look at that same face and feel empathetic for this depressed person. The data is the same, but wildly different reactions are possible.

This chapter is about teaching you how to identify the twelve cognitive distortions that contribute heavily to approval craving in particular. These distortions do this by rendering you helpless to see matters from another viewpoint. When you are ruled by these cognitive distortions, you feel inadequate, impotent, dependent, paranoid, hopeless, and depressed. These distorted styles of thinking lead you to interpret events in your relationships in such a way that you lose your "self." Whenever you are motivated by distorted thoughts, you are unable to make good decisions with regard to your relationships, you allow yourself to be taken advantage of, and so on. This chapter will help you identify and modify these twelve common distorted thought patterns.

Identifying your own distorted thought patterns and styles of thinking might take you less than a week, but creating the automatic habit of identifying these distorted thoughts when they crop up and determining the appropriate behavior throughout the day will take longer.

Many of the following twelve most common irrational beliefs that lead to approval craving seem to overlap. Their differences are not glaringly obvious—being more a matter of nuance and focus of behavior—but they are substantively different.

### 1. *Mental Editing*

You are focusing on one part of an entire situation to the exclusion of everything else. You color the entire situation by the single detail you have selected.

Marcia, a thirty-nine-year-old secretary, reported hypersensitivity to any evidence of loss or rejection, which came to a head when her boyfriend told her he wanted to spend more time with his friends. Marcia experienced his desire to be with friends as a loss of interest in her. She failed to take into account the many positive behaviors he'd demonstrated toward her throughout the relationship—all of the wonderful times they'd been sharing—and simply focused on this single detail: the fact that he wanted to spend time with his friends. She concluded that he didn't love her, didn't care about her, and was becoming bored with the relationship. She exaggerated her fears and focused on them rather than on the entire relationship.

### 2. Black-and-White Thinking

When you think in absolutes, you miss the nuances, the grays of life. You insist on making dichotomous choices, think in extreme measures, and view people as either bad or good, with no room for middle-ground thinking. If someone isn't the perfect partner, he's a terrible partner. Of course, your self-judgments are equally extreme: you are either a saint or a devil.

Clara, a fifty-year-old housewife, felt extremely intimidated by her hypercritical husband. She consulted me after a particularly painful incident in which he and his mother berated her for an unsuccessful Thanksgiving dinner she'd prepared for the family. Clara was ordinarily a good cook, but for this occasion she'd tried a few daring culinary experiments that, in the family's eyes, were untraditional and therefore failures. Clara concluded from the feedback of only one particular incident that she was a terrible entertainer, a terrible cook, and a terrible wife, even though she'd cooked thousands of delicious meals in the past.

### 3. Circumstantial Evidence

In this distorted thinking style, you make sweeping conclusions founded on a single piece of evidence. For example, if you were sick once on an airplane trip, you will never take an airplane trip again.

Sage, a thirty-two-year-old dancer, felt anxious the last time her husband took a business trip. She'd had a history of approval-seeking problems with her husband, in terms of worry over pleasing him. At first she complained only about her anxiety when he'd gone to a business convention. What would happen to her now that he'd taken a position that would require him to travel often? The last time he'd gone away, she'd taken many tranquilizers and visited a psychiatrist. She'd convinced herself that for the rest of her life she would suffer whenever her husband had to leave on extended business. "Everytime he goes away, I'll be desperately unhappy and have panic attacks." Sage was ignoring contrary evidence. The truth was that she'd stayed alone in the past without experiencing panic attacks. By making these generalizations based on little evidence, Sage placed herself in a vulnerable position in terms of her relationship with her husband. His presence in her life and approval of her became much more important.

This distortion—making a leap from circumstantial evidence of one or two incidents to sweeping generalization—leads to a progressively constrained life-style wherein you believe these absolutistic statements as if they are a law governing your chances for happiness. If you find yourself using the following key words, you might well be engaging in this distortion: never, none, always, and everybody.

### 4. Mental Telepathy

Remember the old mnemonic: "When you assume, you make an *ass* out of *U* (you) and *me*." Whenever you are engaging in this cognitive distortion, you are misusing intuition; you believe something because it *seems* right. You have a hunch and you assume that you know. You imagine that everyone reacts the same way without really checking it out. Naturally, you make assumptions about the way others are reacting to you, and usually these assumptions are negative and untested.

Gail, an attorney, was raised in a hypercritical family that demanded 100 percent from her. She developed into an extremely judgmental person, of others and of herself, and set high standards few could meet. When she consulted me she was convinced that her boyfriend, whom she loved a great deal, was constantly finding fault with her intellect. He was also very bright—a literary giant. She felt insecure in conversation with him, uncomfortable in the presence of his friends and colleagues, and constantly overcompensated for what she believed was his view of her deficient intellect. Actually, Gail was projecting onto her boyfriend and his associates her own negative view of herself. To avoid the imagined rejection, Gail attended classes in which she really had no interest, and read papers that held no attraction for her. When her boyfriend joined Gail for a joint therapy session, he was amazed that she harbored these feelings. If anything, he tired of the phoney intellects in his life and appreciated her straightforward manner. Gail had mental-

telepathesized, had made assumptions about her boyfriend's opinion of her intellect and then became miserable because of those
assumptions.

### 5. Awfulizing

This distortion is always characterized by the words what if?
When you operate from this belief system, you are always anticipating fearfully what will happen. This distortion is characterized
by a wild imagination, by catastrophic thoughts such as "What if
he meets someone else?," "What if he notices my wrinkles?," or
"What if he gets bored with me?" We encourage people to add the
phrase "So what!" to these sentences. The key here is that you have
a fertile catatrosphic imagination: every situation in your life is
quickly followed by a "what if?" statement whereby you start
tracking all sorts of horrific consequences. If you "awfulize," you
might well have had nervous Nellie parents who were also cata-
strophizers, so you were exposed to this awfulizing thinking early
in life.

Sheila, a forty-eight-year-old advertising executive, was overwhelmed by awfulizing. At work, whenever she was asked for the
simplest presentation and she handed it in, she engaged in wild
"what if?" thinking. She did the same in her relationship with her
latest boyfriend, worrying incessantly about what would happen if
she made a *faux pas*, or if he were to meet someone better. She
would stay close to him at parties, hanging on his elbow, and he did
complain of feeling suffocated by her at times. Sheila was so afraid
of his finding someone else that she convinced herself if she hung
onto him and stayed close by, he wouldn't leave. Sheila's awfulizing
set her way off stride, made her dependent and passive in the
relationship, and allowed her exploitative boyfriend to be even
more so, thereby exacerbating Sheila's approval craving and insecurity.

### 6. Personalization

This distortion turns you into a walking report card; you are
constantly grading yourself in relation to every experience you
have. You constantly compare yourself to others, and everything
that happens around you somehow gets related to yourself. Some-

times you get an A; most often, though, you get an F. Everything is defined as a clue to your worth or value.

Daphne, a thirty-seven-year-old executive secretary, related what she observed of others to herself and kept an ongoing report card on her ratings in these comparisons. She complained of thoughts such as "was her friend receiving more benefits from therapy than she," "is her friend more intelligent," "why is her colleague at work listened to by the boss and she is not?" This thinking made for an extraordinarily insecure person who then became overly dependent on her boyfriend, because she tended to fail in most of these comparisons.

This distorted thinking style weakens you because you are relating everything around you as a clue to your own worth, placing yourself in an extremely vulnerable position in any relationship.

### 7. Responsibility Distortion

This cognitive distortion takes two forms, but both involve your sense of power and control. In the first form of responsibility distortion, you feel controlled by external events: they *happen* to you. You don't believe that you can make much of a difference in the world, and external events are constantly shaping your life. Others are responsible for your joy and pain and for your feelings of self-worth. You deny your personal responsibility in creating your own experience of the world and of yourself.

Morgan was an elementary school teacher who procrastinated on the job, not writing lesson plans and generally not preparing for her classes as she should. When she was caught, she would blame others for criticizing her and, ultimately, for firing her. She felt "they did it" to her. Morgan also had an abusive boyfriend, and she felt helpless to manage the situation, as if it were outside her control. Yet she complained about her boyfriend incessantly to her friends and anyone else who would listen. When we assessed what she did in the relationship, she realized that she never stood up to him. He was a drinker, but Morgan resisted going to Al-Anon to learn how to manage the relationship. She stayed with him, suffered in silence, and placed the blame for her unhappiness with the relationship on his shoulders alone, instead of realizing that she was also responsible, in allowing him to mistreat her.

The second type of responsibility distortion is believing that you have omnipotent control over others. If you don't help everybody in your life, you feel guilty. You somehow feel responsible for everything and everybody, and you are driven by a kind of missionary zeal, ruled by a Florence Nightingale image. If you are powered by the first type of responsibility distortion, you feel as if you are a victim of everyone. If you are governed by the second type of distortion, you feel an overly developed sense of control and responsibility.

Sacha was a student nurse who'd been dating a young man for several months. He habitually dumped all of his problems on Sacha: his drinking, family troubles, and his fiscal irresponsibility and gambling. She spent most of her waking hours trying to help him and felt guilty when she was unable to. Sacha even felt guilty that she wasn't fulfilling her role based on his expectations— taking care of his problems.

### 8. *The Distortion of Decency*

If you are subject to this belief system, you have developed an idiosyncratic notion of fairness. In couples, we often see one person believing that he or she is behaving fairly, whereas the partner is always unfair. Fairness is basically a subjective assessment of what is needed or hoped for, or of what is being provided by another. This distortion takes various thought forms: "If he cared, he'd come home right after work." But just because he doesn't come immediately home from work doesn't mean he's being unfair. If your behavior is driven by this distortion of decency, you believe your life would be much better if only others treated you fairly.

Jane would repeatedly tell me, "If he really cared, then my husband would listen to me as I listen to him." Like many others, Jane had made hidden bargains with her partner: "If I do this for him, then it's only fair that he returns the favor in *this* way."

### 9. *Emotional Reasoning*

At the core of this distortion is the idea that what you are feeling inside must be valid. If you are feeling something, it must be objectively true. If you feel hurt and ugly, then he must have hurt you and you must be ugly. You believe your emotions are accurate reflections of an objective reality, and everyone should view the world the way you *feel* it. The negative beliefs you have about yourself and others must be true because they *feel* true. The bottom-line difficulty here is that emotions, in and of themselves, really don't have any validity. Many therapists and New Age people stress the importance of tuning into your feelings and trusting and acting on your feelings. But sometimes feelings can't be trusted because they are only products of thinking. If you have mixed-up, automatic, distorted thoughts and beliefs, your emotions are likely to reflect these distortions.

Virginia constantly felt angry at Jim, and concluded that he must be manipulating her, particularly around family issues. Jim always wanted Virginia to visit his family rather than hers, and she felt increasingly angry over the years. In a joint therapy session, Jim revealed that he didn't feel he was manipulating his wife at all. He felt he was fair because they both agreed that his family was far more warm and generous than Virginia's, and whenever she asked him to visit her family, he would do so willingly.

Virginia's anger was really a reflection of her own feelings of inadequacy and anger with her own family. She would project this anger onto Jim, then discover what she was doing, feel guilty, and beg his forgiveness. This pattern put Virginia into a dependent cycle with her husband. I worked with Virginia to help her not necessarily trust her feelings. Her anger was coming from a different place than she thought.

### 10. *The Pressure Fallacy*

This distortion leads you to believe that when you exert pressure or control on another person, it will result in people changing significantly in the direction you demand. You focus all of your attention on others in order to get them to somehow meet your needs. You don't spend much attention or energy on changing your own bad habits, but you're constantly trying to change the behaviors of others through blaming, withholding, and punishing them one way or another. Couples often dig in and try to change each other. The underlying distortion is, "My happiness can only be achieved if I'm able to change other people's behaviors." The reality is that your happiness depends on numerous other choices you make throughout your life, and it's largely *undetermined* by whether or not other people in your life make personal changes. In fact, they certainly won't make major changes when you push hard. They usually dig in.

Pam, a forty-two-year-old airline attendant, was very manipulative in trying to get her boyfriend Fred to change his bad habits; in particular, his drinking. She'd be very indirect, punitive, withhold sex, blame him, attack him, challenge him, and criticize him. She'd throw all sorts of additional criticisms his way. Fred resisted it all. When she came into therapy and went to Al-Anon, she learned to take personal responsibility for her life. It was fine for her to be authentic and direct about what she wanted and to communicate that to Fred, but she had to go on to take charge of her own life, to develop her own friends and interests. She had to stop investing so much time and energy in changing this man who didn't want to be changed.

### 11. *Musturbating*

The internationally renowned psychologist Albert Ellis has called this thinking style "musturbating," based on the (humorous) notion that masturbating is good but musturbating is bad. Essentially this distortion leads you to live your life according to a list of "musts" or "shoulds," highly inflexible demands and rules about how others and you ought to behave in life. If you are an approval craver, you are most likely a victim of shoulds because you believe that by following them you ensure approval and love from your partner and others. Shoulds include "I should be able to find a quick solution to any crisis in my life," "I should never feel hurt," "I should always be happy and cheerful," "I should never feel anger or envy," "I should love my children equally," "I should never make mistakes," "I should never get tired," "I should always look perfect," "I should always behave perfectly," "I must never make demands," "I should be the perfect lover," and "I should always be courageous and brave." The list is endless.

Shoulds create ceaseless, harsh judging, of others and yourself. Your rules about how life should be lived are inflexible and you allow for no compromise or flexibility.

Barbara never allowed herself to feel hurt. A beautiful, thirty-eight-year-old account executive, Barbara was always immaculate and perfectly put together. She presented herself in therapy as someone who was well defended. Barbara complained that she never allowed herself to feel hurt in her relationship with her husband. Whenever her husband, Eric, was insensitive, Barbara would pretend not to feel hurt. Her father had taught Barbara to keep a stiff upper lip, and her mother had an extremely polished image. Although the family was middle-class, they lived in an extremely affluent neighborhood, and the parents were insecure about their social positions. Their insecurity was passed onto Barbara, along with the need to perform perfectly and not to show hurt. The rule was: You just don't show that anything gets to you. Years of not showing hurt to her husband drove Barbara to my office with a massive depression. Her relationship was sour, but she'd never expressed her annoyances and pain.

### 12. *Divine Intervention*

With this cognitive distortion, you feel compelled to always do the proper and correct thing in the hopes of accumulating good acts that will win you divine justice. Then your life will go as you wish. In the extreme, you may feel that you should be rewarded from God, but, more to the point, you want to be rewarded by those in your life whom you want to appreciate you. You work hard, and slave away day and night, hoping your husband will appreciate you or your children will respect, love, and obey you. Very often this leads to the "martyr syndrome," wherein you go on and on, feeling upset that you're not appreciated but continuing to peck away despite your increasing anger at a world that just doesn't deliver the payoff you believe is yours.

Sharon, a twenty-eight-year-old real estate saleswoman, had become the perfect Stepford wife in expectation of rewards from her husband. Everything in the house was immaculate, the children were perfectly cared for, and her grooming was impeccable, but

Sharon constantly complained in therapy, "Why doesn't he appreciate me? Why doesn't he see I'm doing the right thing? When is he going to acknowledge me?" Sharon's husband simply had never learned the language of expressing appreciation, and all the while Sharon's hostility and depression continued to mount.

Look through the previous cognitive distortions carefully. See if any ring true for you. You may add some of your own.

A number of these distortions are drawn from the work of other cognitive therapists, including Albert Ellis's *How to Stop Making Yourself Miserable About Anything,* Aaron Beck's *Cognitive Therapy of Depression,* David Burns's *Feeling Good,* and *Thoughts and Feelings* by Matthew McKay, Martha Davis, and Patrick Fanning.

In order to ensure that you know whether or not you are experiencing these distortions, there are a couple of cardinal signs that can alert you to the awareness that you are engaging in this type of distorted thinking:

♦ *Experiencing painful emotions: anger, depression, anxiety, intense jealousy, intense fearfulness, and intense self-condemnation. Any of these emotions typically signal that one or several distortions are operating.*

♦ *An ongoing conflict or an unresolved or painful phase you are undergoing with a spouse or a significant other.*

## How to Combat Distorted Thinking Patterns

Each of the previously reviewed distorted thoughts can be challenged by a corrective belief pattern.

### 1. *Mental Editing*

You must refocus your thinking and avoid exaggeration. Incorporate thoughts such as, "This incident does not represent the entire situation; it is only one small aspect of my relationship with this person." In Marcia's case, she must attend to the positive times she's shared with her boyfriend and view his desire to be with friends as a reflection of his personableness and caring nature. Marcia should check her magnification and use of hyperbole: "What he's doing is terrible!" and "I can't take it." Most human beings can "take it"; they are capable of handling numerous misfortunes in their lives.

### 2. Black-and-White Thinking

To correct this mistaken cognition, you must resist making absolutistic judgments. Recognize that people exist along a continuum, and try to think in terms of percentages. For example, "Ten percent of the time I prepare a poor meal, and I will no longer avoid cooking for company because of fear of disapproval."

Clara, our fifty-year-old housewife, was urged to keep a log for about three months that recorded the general reactions to the meals she made. She was able to discover that only a small percentage of her meals received negative reviews.

### 3. Circumstantial Evidence

Quantify, rather than use hyperbole and exaggeration. Examine all of the evidence closely, almost as if you were an investigating detective, before you come to your conclusion. Does the evidence lead to my conclusion that the situation is as dismal and hopeless as I feel? Challenge absolutistic words and phrases such as "always," "never," and "I must." Substitute phrases such as "It would be nice" and "I would prefer." Sage's notion that "I won't be able to stand being alone when my husband goes away" is erroneous. When she actually reviews the evidence—what really happened the last ten times she was alone—she will realize that she did survive the experiences well. A good cognitive corrective would be, "I would need more convincing proof before I accept that I have to always feel badly in this particular situation."

### 4. Mental Telepathy

The key here is to make no inferences. All intuitions are hypotheses to be tested. A good cognitive corrective would be, "My feelings are my own, not necessarily shared by others." Gail has to check out her assumption that her boyfriend is embarrassed by her lack of intellect. She should ask him if he is, indeed, embarrassed, and examine if there really is evidence for him to make such a conclusion, to see if there are alternative ways of understanding why he might be ignoring her or not discussing highly intellectual matters with her.

### 5. Awfulizing

Anxious people suffer from awfulizing, which translates as viewing matters as more than 100-percent bad. Very little in life is more than 100-percent bad. Perhaps intense, chronic, physical pain over months or years with no relief or no hope of relief qualifies, but little else does. Check out the realistic odds. What is the real probability that these awful scenarios you imagine actually will occur? Has anybody ever told you they will occur? Is there any reason to believe they will occur? Systematic desensitization, to be discussed in a later chapter, is helpful in reducing awfulizing anxiety.

Sheila was encouraged to purposefully engage in faux pas in front of her boyfriend in order to convince herself that these social errors would not automatically prompt him to find another woman. The faux pas she chose was to talk and dance with other men at a party, a behavior clinging-vine Sheila would ordinarily have never engaged in before. Not only did her boyfriend not dump her, he became more solicitous and possessive of her and Sheila developed greater self-confidence.

### 6. Personalization

Again, check everything out and draw no conclusions without proof. Abandon the habit of making comparisons between yourself and others. One helpful technique is called thought stopping.

Daphne, who constantly report-carded herself—that is, constantly graded herself in comparison to others—was asked to make note of the incidents in which she did this. Each night she was to review these incidents and say the word *stop* aloud to herself at each unfavorable comparison. She would then drop the thought of comparing herself unfavorably to someone else, and switch the thought to a more appropriate one of viewing that person's success with a passive, loving, caring attitude.

Thought stopping allows you to interrupt comparing yourself

unfavorably to another—that is, personalizing everything. Repeat the thought-stopping process every evening with every thought of unfavorable comparison during the day, until you simply stop engaging in this futile behavior.

Comparisons are a risky gamble. Sometimes you win, sometimes you lose. Losing can sink you into a deep funk, but you can never be the most attractive, intelligent, talented, loved person on the planet. Ultimately, comparisons are a no-win situation.

### 7. Responsibility Distortion

If you feel externally controlled , you must realize that you make things happen, and that you do have control over the specific choices you make every day—choices that determine your fate. Very little other than hurricanes and other acts of God are totally out of your control. To believe you lack any control is absurd. Once you recognize that it's you who is making the choices for your health, your relationships, your career, and so on, you must ask yourself, "How can I change those poor choices?" Most likely it's the choices that are creating difficulty in your life.

Morgan, a teacher, received assertiveness training in therapy and went through standard role-playing exercises. She learned to express her annoyance to her drinking boyfriend, and regularly attended Al-Anon meetings. She also learned to deal with her procrastination about lesson plans and truly began to "own" responsibility for when they were supposed to be handed in.

Sacha, who feels omnipotent—responsible for her boyfriend's problems—must realize that we cannot overcome another's pain. Only that person can make that change. Compassion and a slavish adherence to the notion that you must help are opposing ideas. People grow most by working out problems for themselves; often we have to allow them to do that.

### 8. The Distortion of Decency

The notion of fairness or decent behavior can be too subjective to be invoked as a judgment. Drop the notion of fairness completely. Often the notion of fairness is a disguise for people to express their wants, desires, demands, and requirements. They posit the notion of fairness in order to get others to capitulate.

Jane was taught to recognize that her husband had never "signed" onto her bargain. "He *should* be fair to me, as I am to him." She realized it was important for him to hang out occasionally with the boys. He didn't feel he was being unfair and that he had already made many other sacrifices and compromises for the sake of the relationship. Jane learned that she was using the concept of "fairness" in a self-serving way, and she dropped it.

### 9. *Emotional Reasoning*

Feelings are often false reflections of reality, based almost completely on thoughts. Your feelings will also lack validity if the thoughts that create them are not valid. The key is to be skeptical about your feelings. Examine them closely and make sure they are not merely responses to distorted thoughts. If I say I feel like a kangaroo, that doesn't make me a kangaroo. If I feel foolish, that doesn't mean I am foolish.

When Virginia realized that her anger was not really about Joe, her husband, but about hidden agendas regarding her family and how they had treated her for years, she was able to confront them and work through her misdirected rage.

### 10. *The Pressure Fallacy*

Take responsibility for your own happiness. Since people are resistant to change, stop trying to force people into changing in order to give you what you want and need. Find the right set of choices to follow in order to make your life a happier one. A good corrective cognition would be, "My happiness essentially depends on all of the choices I make throughout my life, and I make them for myself. Asking people to make changes in order to ensure my happiness is very tricky and can be unfair and unrealistic."

Pam, our airline attendant, quickly learned that she had numerous interests and talents she had not pursued previously. She had been using her frustration with trying to change Fred as an excuse for not improving the quality of her own life.

### 11. *Musturbating*

Develop looser rules and mores; try to be more flexible in your thinking and expectations. Drop words such as should, ought, and must from your vocabulary. Become an aspiring personality rather than a requiring personality. The aspiring person says things such as "I would prefer," "It would be nice," and "I will work hard to make this happen." The requiring person says things such as "It must be this way," "I can't stand it if it's not," "It ought to be," "It should be," and "I demand it be this way." What cosmic rule suggests that "it" should be the way you demand it to be? Also, think of exceptions to the rules you construct. Barbara had to recognize that when she really examined the situation, there were many exceptions to the shoulds that had guided her life.

12. *Divine Intervention*

You accept pain and travail in the expectation that your good acts will be rewarded at some future date. You must recognize that heaven is a long way off. Ask yourself if you want others to deliver this payoff to you in a way they will ultimately resent. The reinforcement and reward is now, not off in the distant future. Act in a self-reinforcing way today rather than martyr yourself in the expectation of justice to come. Sharon learned that if you perform good acts for others, do so because you want to, not for a reward somewhere down the road.

Review the previous corrective cognitions carefully because these healthy thoughts and beliefs are your greatest weapon in combating your approval craving and fear of rejection. The chart will help you use these improved thoughts to systematically dismantle your approval craving. Use the chart whenever you are feeling particularly upset or are locked in a painful, apparently unresolvable conflict with your partner or love object.

## Challenging Your Faulty Thoughts

The following instructions correspond to the numbered heads of the chart.

1. Name the emotion you are feeling. It could be fear, anger, anxiety, jealousy, depression, and so on.

2. Describe the situation going on right now that is eliciting that emotion.
3. From the list of twelve, choose the distorted thought creating the emotion.
4. Rewrite the distorted thought in your own words to help you better identify it.
5. Write the rational challenge to your distorted thought.
6. Describe the change in your approval-craving behavior that you predict will result from doing steps one through five.

## Challenge Chart

1. *Emotion:* _____

   _____

   _____

   _____

2. *Situation:* _____

   _____

   _____

   _____

3. *Distorted Thought:* _____

   _____

   _____

   _____

4. *Personalized Thought:* _____

   _____

   _____

   _____

5. *Challenge:* _____

_____

_____

_____

6. *Change:* _____

_____

*Notes:* _____

_____

_____

_____

CHAPTER 4

# DO YOU CRAVE APPROVAL FROM EVERYONE?

## *TAKING STOCK OF YOUR APPROVAL-CRAVING BEHAVIORS ON THE JOB, AND WITH STRANGERS, THE FAMILY, AND FRIENDS*

♦

In this chapter we take stock of three other major contexts of approval craving. As we have suggested several times in previous chapters, approval craving occurs not just with romantic partners. It most likely also manifests in other important areas of your life. Approval craving can be a broader, more pervasive problem than you realize.

If you have discovered your approval craving within your relationship, you probably need to take a look at other aspects of your life. In order to achieve lasting change, you must modify the distorted thinking that creates approval craving in all aspects of your life, not just romantic situations. If you don't examine your entire being in many types of situations and only work on assertiveness with your intimate partner, you will only be going through the motions. You will make some changes, but you will not learn principles that will affect you positively throughout your life, and your chances for relapsing are increased.

This book is not a primer on assertiveness training. Many other sources are available to do just that. (One of the best is *Don't Say Yes When You Mean to Say No* by Herbert Fensterheim and Jean Baer.) Approval craving, however, is closely related to assertiveness difficulties, so this chapter also teaches you how to be more assertive in your thinking and behavior in relating to strangers, work peers, and family and friends. In my clinical practice, assertiveness deficiencies and social anxiety are the most common problems presented. At least 50 percent of our patients report inability to communicate their needs and fear of social situations. We have noticed over the years that our approval-craving clients also suffer from these generalized assertiveness deficiencies.

Many experts have defined assertiveness. Dr. Arnold Lazarus, one of the first to construct a definition, isolated four criteria: (1) the ability to say no without candy-coating it, (2) the ability to make demands and requests of others, (3) the ability to begin, maintain, and end general conversations, and (4) the ability to express the full range of emotions, from anger to joy, from sadness to euphoria. Dr. Alberti and Dr. Emmons, in *Your Perfect Right*, state that "assertive behavior promotes equality in human relationships, enabling us to act in our own best interests, to stand up for ourselves without undue anxiety, to express feelings honestly and comfortably, and to exercise personal rights without denying the rights of others."

You can see how these definitions relate closely to the notion of anxiety about rejection and approval craving. Learning how to be assertive helps you escape from your sense of powerlessness. At the Institute for Behavorial Therapy, we've spent years teaching people how to stand up for their rights, how to communicate their needs directly and authentically, and how to learn to say no—all in an attempt to allow them feel more self-confident, to be willing to take more risks, and, ultimately, to learn that they don't necessarily need the blessing or approval or love of others in order to feel good about themselves and to get along in the world. It's not enough to learn that you don't need approval craving. It's not even enough to change your belief systems or cognitions, reviewed in the previous chapter. You also have to *behave* more assertively. Change comes about when we *behave ourselves* into feeling and thinking differently.

As discussed earlier, fear of negative evaluation is the link between lack of assertiveness and approval craving. Approval cravers fear negative evaluation more than anything. Fear of rejection by others or not being liked or approved of is also the hallmark of the unassertive person who fails to act because he fears the consequences of looking foolish, making a mistake, or being unpopular.

In the diagnostic and statistical manual of the American Psychiatric Association, social anxiety is defined as "a persistent fear of social situations in which the person is exposed to possible scrutiny by others and fears that he might do something humiliating or embarrassing."

The following is a fear-of-rejection checklist. Read through the following sentences and make a minus sign next to the item that creates in you feelings of rejection or fear or depression. Place a plus sign by the items you feel you can handle assertively. This exercise will help you realize in what ways you fear rejection.

_____ A close friend or employer says you have not performed a job adequately.

_____ Your application for a position at an organization is turned down.

_____ Someone neglects to congratulate you on a promotion.

_____ You've asked someone to get information for you that you cannot obtain, and she says she is unable to do this.

_____ You and a friend make a new acquaintance and they seem more interested in conversing with each other than with you.

_____ You are at dinner with people you just met, and they are sharing jokes and stories about past experiences together.

_____ In a classroom, you answer the professor's question to the class and you feel ignored.

_____ You are interested in dating someone, but they do not show reciprocal interest.

_____ A friend asks you to do a favor that would be on the shady side of legality. You know you should refuse.

_____ You return a damaged garment to a store and the clerk accuses you of being too picky or of having worn the garment and damaged it yourself.

_____ You need to ask a friend for a loan of one hundred dollars, but as you start to ask, he complains of some bills he's got to pay soon.

_____ A friend betrays a confidence and tells you that you're being overly sensitive.

Those individuals who are truly unconcerned about rejection will have marked between ten and twelve of the items with a plus sign. If you have more negative than plus signs, your concern about rejection is far too great. Keep reading. This chapter is for you.

One reason criticism can hurt you so much is the element of surprise. When criticism is unexpected, it hurts more than if you've had time to anticipate and prepare for it. In preparing for criticism or rejection, you should know that there are three types: valid, put-downs, and unrealistic criticism.

Unrealistic criticism is utterly silly, without any basis in truth. For example, someone could notice a solitary pimple on your face and accuse you of neglecting your appearance and health. Put-downs may contain some element of truth, but they are expressed in a hurtful way. For example, someone could say, "You have a pimple; it really looks disgusting." Valid or legitimate criticism reflects the truth, is stated honestly, assertively, but is not negatively judgmental. "I'm concerned about that pimple on your face. It looks like it may get infected."

The first type of criticism, the silly one, should be discounted. When it comes to put-downs, consider the source. There may be an element of truth, but what is the person's hidden agenda? Learn to listen honestly and openly to the feedback you receive from valid criticism.

Most of us go through life without ever asking anyone, "How'm

I doing?"—mostly because we're afraid of hearing an honest answer. If you're an approval craver, you suspect that you have inadvertently goofed in some terrible way, and you just don't want to know about it. But you will never really know how someone else is evaluating you, and you will miss the opportunity to learn from your mistakes. The giving and getting of feedback is essential if you are ever to achieve real intimacy with another person. Another reason to prepare yourself to learn from feedback, including criticism, is that feedback is essential on the job. Being a willing recipient of feedback says to your colleagues and boss that you are interested in your work and committed to doing well.

If you are an approval craver, you are terrified of the prospect of criticism. You are doing whatever you can to disarm the potential criticizer. In every situation, you anticipate criticism and rejection, and do whatever you can to head it off. Preparing yourself by understanding and discriminating among the three types of criticism, and by learning to solicit helpful feedback, will help you rid yourself of your fear of criticism and the rejection you believe it inevitably brings.

As you learn to be more assertive in your life, you will be able to look forward to several new and rewarding experiences. As an assertive person, you will do the following.

♦ *Avoid justifying every opinion.*

Every time Connie offers her opinion on a subject and someone suggests a counteropinion, she either appeals to another source, such as a book, or resorts to phrases such as "Many people believe this." She must call in support from higher authorities.

♦ *Learn to speak up for your rights.*

You will be able to say things such as "I believe it's my turn now," "I asked you to give me ten dollars worth of gas, not ten dollars and fifty cents; it's your fault you weren't here to turn the pump off."

Chloe will often sit on her annoyance and privately rail against the unfairness of having someone cut in line in front of her long after the insult occurred.

♦ *Learn to ask why.*

When someone asks you to do something that strikes you either as not legitimate, unnecessary, or displeasing, you can question why you should do it.

Stephanie's boyfriend continues to ask her to place illegal bets with a bookie, something with which she is very uncomfortable. But she is fearful that expressing that fear will garner his disapproval.

♦ *Accept compliments*

You will accept compliments without making self-disparaging remarks or openly disagreeing.

Twenty-nine-year-old Sandra, a beauty shop operator, was very concerned that everyone like her. Whenever anyone complimented her on her appearance, she would always denigrate it. "Oh, this old thing?" she would say. Or "I got a real bargain on this outfit! It was only twenty dollars." Or "Oh no, I'm a mess today." That behavior ultimately punishes the compliment giver, who feels put down.

♦ *Learn to use* feeling *talk.*

You will be able to describe your feelings about a situation rather than giving only a factual response. "I really feel uncomfortable about you being late all the time" is preferable to feeling rejected and pouting.

Alice would intellectually describe how her friend should keep a watch handy in order to avoid lateness, or talk about why the first few minutes of a movie are so important. But she was reluctant to share her annoyance about the friend's lateness through the use of true, authentic feeling talk.

♦ *Learn to be persistent.*

In pursuing a work-related raise, Laurel learned to feel justified in insisting that her boss meet with her on several occasions after he rejected the idea. She simply would not take no for an answer. Joan, a freelance graphics designer, learned to be persistent in her pursuit of work, to let no one cause her to give up completely.

One of the main criticisms over the years of assertiveness training is that it is manipulative. But manipulation is a pejorative term meaning trying to control someone else's behavior by underhanded means and often for some hidden motives. Assertiveness training avoids such underhanded means to promote change in another, and instead promotes aboveboard contracts between you and another based on genuine communication of exactly what the positive consequences will be if they change their behavior. Assertiveness training takes into account the needs and desires of the person with whom you are interacting. It does not mean bullying or plunging ahead; it means honest, genuine regard for the feelings of another.

## How Does the Approval Craver Learn to Be More Assertive?

The first step is to keep a diary of your interactions, an ongoing record of any interpersonal situations that occur that cause you to feel more than only slightly uncomfortable. The discomfort can take the form of depression, anxiety, fear, a surge of needing approval, or jealousy. Whenever you experience a powerful emotion during the day, pull out your diary and answer the following questions:

- With whom did this situation occur?
- When?
- What were we talking about?
- Where did the situation occur?
- What specifically did the other person do or say?
- What specifically did I do or fail to do, or say or fail to say?
- What automatic thoughts or cognitive distortions did I engage in? (See Chapter 3.)
- Did I experience any signs of tension: perspiration, heart pounding, giggling, breathing difficulty, butterflies in the stomach, tension in the neck and shoulders, dry mouth, and so on.
- What is my assertion goal in this situation?
- How important is it to my happiness to change this situation? If I assert myself and challenge my approval craving, how

likely is it that I will change the situation for the long term? Will the change be only short-term, or is there a reasonable possibility that the change will be permanent?

• What might the other person do in response to my more assertive behavior?

• Are there any genuinely negative consequences for asserting myself?

The following are reasons why keeping this diary is so essential to changing your approval-craving behaviors.

First, it calls behaviors and cognitions into awareness. So much of our approval craving and unassertiveness is done pretty much without our awareness. We don't stop and watch ourselves. Our lives are not like snapshots; they're like movies, ongoing. This diary makes your life a bit more like a snapshot, where you can stop and appraise exactly what you're doing.

Second, so much of overcoming approval craving has to do with identifying and modifying faulty cognitions and identifying and modifying faulty behaviors. By keeping this diary, you can identify which behaviors and cognitions need to be changed. Then you can work to modify them.

This diary will begin training your ability to identify situations that continue to be a problem. Particular themes will come into focus. In other words, are you particularly unassertive with friends, an employer, strangers, or a family member? Are there certain situations that are problematic: being interviewed, protesting someone's annoying habit, presenting an idea, returning merchandise, being at a party, or giving directions?

Later in this chapter we will discuss role playing as an important technique in learning assertive behaviors. The information gleaned from your diary will be an invaluable tool for recreating situations, as well as practicing and rehearsing new behaviors, cognitions, and responses that need to be learned in order to overcome your approval craving.

Phelps and Austin, in *The Assertive Woman*, suggest that there are four distinct considerations in saying no. First, you must decide clearly whether or not the other person's request of you is reasonable. If you find yourself uncomfortable or hedging, it may be a clue that you really want to refuse.

Second, sometimes you need more information from the person before deciding whether or not you want to say no. Approval cravers, in particular, have difficulty saying, "I need more time to get more information," or "Please give me more information," or "I'm not sure about this." They fear possible rejection.

Third, practice saying a simple no, without excuses, justifications, candy-coating, and explanations. Brief explanations are reasonable, but approval cravers, out of a fear of angering someone, will go on and on about why they must refuse this request. We often have approval cravers practice saying no in front of a mirror, all the while observing their body language. Often you will find you say no with an apologetic smile or with downcast eyes, so that a different message is conveyed. You can also practice with a friend whom you've asked to make requests of you. In group therapy, we have patients make requests to each other, with the partner repeatedly saying no.

Fourth, learn to say no without saying "I'm sorry, but. . . ." The words I'm sorry often make your position vulnerable. You lack conviction and people can exploit what they sense is your guilt.

## Approval Craving on the Job

Other than love relationships, nowhere is it more frightening to assert yourself than in a job situation because our work egos are so fragile. We tend to define ourselves so much based on how well we are doing at work, if our colleagues like us, whether or not we get promotions, and how we are evaluated by our supervisors. More and more companies have been embracing the notion of assertiveness. I have given many seminars on assertiveness training in the corporate world, teaching workers to be more direct and authentic in their communications. Some companies are still fearful of assertiveness, mistakenly believing this will lead to wholesale mutiny. But most companies realize that individuals who feel they have direct access to express their gripes will be happier, more productive, and harmonious employees in the end and won't engage in passive-aggressive sabotaging behaviors.

Every company has its own philosophy. You must recognize that some companies encourage assertiveness, whereas others discourage it. Many signs can be read to determine where your company stands. Is assertiveness rewarded at your place of business? Are there incentives for independent behavior on the job? Or does your supervisor seem to avoid listening to your ideas about improving the company or the department's performance, saying that this is the task of management, not yours.

Look for these signals within the company to determine whether or not they will be responsive to your assertiveness. In general, though, assertiveness promotes self-respect, and if you respect yourself, you respect your work and perform more effectively.

Go back to your diary and see what types of assertiveness situations have come up on the job. What cognitive distortions did you identify? Certain types of situations tend to arise in the work arena. There are four set steps for handling them.

### ♦ Problem Area 1

A common problem area for many approval cravers is requesting information. For example, you may have asked your supervisor several times to instruct you in the new computer so that you can carry out an assigned project.

### ♦ Corrective Steps

*Step 1: Detail the situation.* "I've asked you several times to instruct me in this program so that I can do this job. You've assured me you would a number of times, but you haven't taken any action yet."

*Step 2: Reveal your feelings.* "I'm really troubled because I'm not being exposed to an important part of my job. I'm feeling more frustrated daily, and I find myself becoming resentful."

*Step 3: Pinpoint your goal.* "I want you to tell me exactly when you'll be available to instruct me on this new program or tell me who in the department can, and when they can help me."

*Step 4: Results.* "If you do teach me this program, I believe I will be able to save this department quite a bit of money over the next six months. If I'm not taught it soon, then I'm just going to end up wasting a good deal of time by working on other, much less important projects."

◆ *Problem Area 2*
Another universal problem for approval cravers in the workplace is requesting a raise after one has been implicitly promised but not yet given.

◆ *Corrective Steps*
*Step 1: Detail the situation.* "I've been at this company for over a year and was promised an evaluation for a merit raise a month ago. I believe I'm making a good deal less than others with comparable experience."

*Step 2: Reveal your feelings.* "I believe I'm not getting the fairest treatment, though I've made significant contributions to this department's success."

*Step 3: Pinpoint your goals.* "Can we arrange a time on Friday afternoon when you're done with that important meeting to discuss my raise in more detail?"

*Step 4: Results.* "If we are able to work this out, I look forward to a number of years of enjoying my work here and making a contribution. But, quite frankly, I cannot imagine staying on indefinitely unless I feel my work is being appreciated in a financial way."

## *Approval Craving from Friends and Family*

Approval cravers are terrified that if they garner disapproval from these people who have been constant in their lives, these people will disappear. Many of my clients have told me they genuinely felt that if they angered a good friend or family member, that friend or relative would just drop away forever. One of the distortions operating here is that the friend or family member will negate all of the wonderful years of friendship, all of the warm, shared experiences because of a single incident. Occasionally this does happen, but more often than not, good friends and family are able to overlook single incidents and talk things out.

In a 1971 article, Margaret Adams wrote about "the compassion trap," one that is exclusive to females who believe their very existence is defined by service to others. They believe they must provide compassion to all at all times.

Phelps and Austin also discuss this issue and list four areas in which women can be trapped by compassion toward friends and family.

First, when a crisis arises, a woman may push aside projects important to her in order to pay full attention to the crisis. She believes she is indispensable.

One young physician who was pursuing important laboratory research actually took off from her work for several weeks at a crucial point in her research because her husband's father had become ill. Sensing that her husband was rather insensitive and unsupportive, she spent all of her time visiting the old man.

Second, she believes no one else is as concerned about a particular problem situation as she is, and, as a woman, she enjoys a special understanding and compassion that others lack.

This young doctor never questioned her husband's negligence of his father. In that she was the woman, she was automatically the nurturing, compassionate one who should give up her pursuits for a needy person.

Third, she may see herself as a protector. As a mother she's afraid to act on her own behalf for fear her children will suffer. Many women who are trapped in unhappy, even abusive, marriages refuse to leave because they don't want to deprive the children of their father. Other women give up their careers to care for aging, ill parents.

Stella, a thirty-eight-year-old social worker, read our first book, *Bailing Out,* and realized she was a victim of the "Pied Piper syndrome," the irrational fear that her children would suffer untold horror if she left her unhappy marriage. Stella had read all of the books detailing the negative consequences for children if their parents divorce without noting the data on the millions of children of divorce who grow up relatively unscathed. But Stella was hunting for evidence that she had to remain the protector at all costs. Even her children begged her to leave the marriage with her controlling, bullying husband, but Stella adamantly refused until she recognized through therapy that not only was she suffering from the Pied Piper syndrome, but from severe approval craving. Stella was concerned that she would lose the approval of friends and family if she left her husband and caused any damage to her children. When she began to recognize her own needs and that she had played the protector role most of her adult life, she was able to make that decision.

Fourth, a woman may be reluctant to leave a job that makes her unhappy because her clients may suffer from her absence. Sheila, a nurse at a small nursing home, is abused by her supervisor. But she returns to the job day after day, because she feels she is indispensable to her patients. If she leaves, they will suffer, even though she knows her colleagues are surely competent and that she could pursue her career further elsewhere.

You may be struggling with other issues surrounding your relations with friends and relatives: being assertive with those who demand personal favors, with those who demand you spend more time with them although their company is unpleasant to you, with those who ask you to participate in what they feel is a worthy cause, with those who impose their political or religious views on you, with parents who treat you like a child, and with friends who demand greater sexual intimacy than you wish to give.

You've maintained your diary and you've identified your ineffective behaviors and distorted beliefs. Identify the problematic situations with friends and family and go through the four-step process: detailing, revealing feelings, pinpointing, and results. Each dialogue you have in similar situations should always include the following:

- An expression of your upset
- A clarification of your expectations of the other person and the goals you desire
- An internal challenging of your disturbed, irrational thoughts

- Preparations for resistance or refusal from the person to go along with your desires or goals by having in your mind an alternative or compromise plan

## *Approval Craving from Strangers*

The following are common themes that arise with strangers.

♦ *Being assertive with repair people who overcharge or who don't do the work properly.*

Approval cravers such as Jan are often very reluctant to call repair people back. She rationalizes that they know better, that they did the best they could. This behavior was particularly evident when a plumber charged her one hundred dollars to fix a toilet tank that did not work properly ten minutes after he had left. For days, she fretted until she and I did a role play that proved to her that she could call the plumber, knowing that she had the right to ask him to redo the work.

♦ *Negotiating expectations for services to be rendered.*

Jan also had many difficulties in gauging exactly what she could expect from service people. She felt great discomfort about determining what else she could ask of the plumber—if she could request he fix other items in the bathroom for the same price. Her overall concern was that he not dislike her.

♦ *Being assertive with high-pressure salespeople.*

Ellen reported to me how she would end up buying unwanted subscriptions to magazines because she didn't know how to say no gracefully, and, particularly, because she didn't want to hurt the feelings of salespeople—some of whom were neighbors and friends of neighbors—and have them think poorly of her. We spent much time teaching her how to say no—how to express appreciation that they thought to ask if she was interested, but that she really wasn't interested in purchasing. Ellen was helped greatly to learn that she could express appreciation for being shown the material, and that she could be appropriately polite as she turned the item down.

♦ *Getting the commercial service you desire, such as from a waiter.*

Patricia would complain constantly that she would often order food a certain way at her local restaurant, yet her requests would not be followed. She often would not feel courageous enough to return it. We did many role plays, getting her to challenge her incorrect distortions of what these people expected of her until she realized that their primary role was to keep her happy, not the reverse, and that she was purchasing a service from them. On a few occasions I actually accompanied her to restaurants and modeled the assertive response of sending food back. Then she and I talked across the table about how she could challenge those interfering distortions: "The waiter won't like me," "I won't get good service from here again," "I want to be welcomed here as a single woman," and so on.

♦ *Getting health care service from busy doctors.*

Elsie, whom I'd been seeing for many years, was a woman in her mid-sixties who had many health-related reasons to visit doctors. She would always leave feeling dissatisfied because many of her questions had not been answered. The doctors always seemed too busy and distracted to deal with her "unimportant" concerns. We worked hard to get Elsie to challenge her distorted beliefs that the doctors would view her complaints as unimportant. I reminded her that she was paying for a service and that any doctor who would be put off or would dislike her because she was asking questions was probably not the best medical person to consult.

♦ *Smiling back when a stranger smiles at you.*

A number of my patients regularly try to overcome their anxiety in public places when someone smiles at them or gives them a pleasant look. Their initial tendency is to turn off and shut down, feeling paranoid or frightened. We've worked on challenging the distorted idea that the person wants to pick you up or has more than a fleeting interest in you, although occasionally that is the case. More often than not, however, the person is just being friendly, wanting to make a connection in the anonymous street.

Again, refer to your diary for problematic situations with strangers. Challenge your distorted beliefs, identify your problem behaviors, engage in feeling talk, if appropriate and then go through the four steps previously described: detailing, revealing, pinpointing, and results.

One particularly problematic area in dealing with strangers is anger and anger control. The approval craver becomes a grievance collector who is always turning the other cheek and not making waves. She continues to stockpile more and more anger and ultimately explodes with rage far out of proportion to the particular situation, or behaves in a backstabbing, passive-aggressive fashion. Novacco, in his landmark book *Anger Control,* emphasizes the importance of rehearsing self-statements to control outbursts of anger. This is particularly important for approval cravers in their dealings with strangers. Because they have not stated their needs for fear of disapproval, approval cravers will often sit on their bad feelings until they become explosive within them, and then will act out in a very angry and inappropriately aggressive fashion, compounding their problems further because the stranger will not understand where the rage is coming from. It seems so misdirected and overreactive. Novacco suggested four steps for self-directed statements that prepare for situations that cause anger. You can close your eyes, clearly imagine the provoking situation, and rehearse some or all of the following thoughts in your mind.

1. *Preparing for Provocation*
Remind yourself: "This is going to upset me, but I know how to deal with it. I can work out a plan to handle this. I can manage this situation and regulate my anger. If I find myself getting upset, I will know what to do. I won't take this too seriously. Easy does it. Remember to maintain your sense of humor."

2. *Reacting During a Confrontation*
Tell yourself: "Stay calm, relax. As long as I keep my cool, I'm in control. Just roll with the punches; don't get bent out of shape. For someone to be that irritable, he must be awfully unhappy. I'm not going to let him get to me. There is no need to doubt myself; what he says doesn't matter."

3. *Coping with Anger Arousal*
Tell yourself: "My muscles are starting to feel tight. Time to relax and slow things down. Getting upset won't help. It's just not

worth it to get so angry. I'll let him make a fool of himself. Time to take a deep breath. My anger is a signal of what I need to do. Time to instruct myself to calm down. He'd probably like me to get really angry. Well, I'm going to disappoint him."

4. *Reflecting on an Experience After It's Over*

If the conflict was unresolved, say to yourself: "Forget about the situation. Thinking about the aggravation only makes you upset. Try to shake it off; don't let it interfere with your day (or evening). Can you laugh about this? It's probably not so serious. Don't take it personally." If the conflict is resolved or if the coping is successful, tell yourself: "I handled that situation pretty well. It wasn't as difficult as I thought. I'm doing better at this all the time. I actually got through this one without becoming angry. My pride can get me into trouble, but when I don't take things too seriously, I'm better off."

# Roadblocks

We wish that when you are learning to discard approval craving the whole world will cooperate and give you what you want. In fact, many with whom you will practice your new assertiveness will set up roadblocks. The following are common roadblocks you will probably encounter.

♦ *The Put-Off Roadblock*

This often occurs on the job. You make a request for a salary increase and a supervisor engages in the "put off" roadblock, where they say "I can't discuss that with you right now."

♦ *The Denying Roadblock*

This might happen with strangers. Someone is pushing their elbow into your side on a bus or subway, and when you ask them to move back, they say, "What are you talking about!"

This pattern is also common with families. Gwen insisted that her husband had promised to take her away for a long weekend. He denied it and made her feel demanding and unreasonable.

### ♦ *The Blaming Roadblock*

This is common in families. You might say, "You never compliment me for my success in business." They might respond, "That's because I'm still angry at you for your overspending." Here your legitimate assertion is deflected with an irrelevant grudge response.

Diehard approval cravers will respond to the roadblocks with an internal "Gee, they're right."

In the matter of the salary increase, they'll think or say, "You're right, it was inappropriate of me to ask for a raise now." The assertive person will persist until the boss comes around.

With the stranger, the approval craver will become embarrassed and apologetic, and think she's being too sensitive and paranoid. The assertive person might say, "I'm sure I didn't imagine it. Please step back."

With the family, the approval craver will tell herself, "He sees that I haven't changed; I do overspend. Big deal, I know how to make money, but I also know how to waste it." The assertive response would be to say, "I feel hurt when you raise old issues. They are not appropriate now."

# CHAPTER 5

# DEVELOPING A
# PHILOSOPHY OF
# SELF-ESTEEM
# THAT LASTS

♦

When he was mayor of New York City, Ed Koch would periodically query his constituents, "How'm I doing?" That was a misguided question for him or anyone to ask without being specific. What we really must do if we are eager to know about our acceptance is to ask, "How am I doing as . . ." and then name a specific role we play. How am I doing as a mayor, as a friend, as a tennis player?

As we will discuss throughout this chapter, self-acceptance is about accepting your self independent of "How I'm doing" in particular aspects of my life. Approval cravers have not learned the importance of noncontingent self-acceptance, whereby we accept ourselves and our being and existence and worthiness quite separate from anything we do.

Approval cravers are notorious self-raters. They are always pulling out report cards on how they are doing. They are always rating themselves, and the evaluation is more often than not overwhelmingly negative. The key is that they rate *themselves,* not their performances. And they are particularly concerned about whether or not the love object approves of them. So they frequently define their own personal worth based on whether the love object accepts or approves of them.

The following equation tells the entire story: He approves of me = I am worthy. He does not approve of me = I am worthless. This is a basic irrational idea, and one of the most important and critical issues in therapy when working with approval cravers. I have to teach them to separate who they are from what they do—from the myriad of talents, assets, and liabilities they possess.

Melissa, a relatively optimistic woman, would come to therapy sessions in a great mood, and report a good state of mind for most of the day. But if her boyfriend criticized her for her cooking or cleaning or her general housekeeping, she would lie awake the entire night, sobbing. She would conclude that *she* had been devalued. She also reported that when her *boyfriend* made a mistake, she would again feel exalted.

Melissa's reaction is common with report card people. They tend to vilify themselves when a personal behavior or trait is criticized. And when the person making the criticism slips up himself, the report carder feels happier, exalted, and special.

Robin was also a relatively happy person, but whenever her husband Sam said she was a poor and inconsistent disciplinarian of their two children, she became depressed and stopped parenting almost completely, withdrawing noticeably from her children. Robin also would sleep with other men during those periods of depression, in order to punish her husband in her mind.

Again, a singular aspect of Robin's personality, her inability to discipline her children consistently, was criticized by her significant other. Robin then generalized this criticism to a total sense of worthlessness.

Justine, another relatively optimistic woman with a successful career as a real estate agent, was criticized for her comparatively more relaxed work habits by her perfectionistic, workaholic husband. Justine would become despondent at his jabs and even entertain thoughts of suicide.

When I appeared on "The Sally Jesse Raphael Show," with women whose husbands had left without any notice or goodbye, each of the panelists denounced herself. "I should have been nicer to him," was the common theme. One woman whose husband had a gambling problem said, "I should have helped him with that problem more." Until I counseled them a bit on the program, not one of the women was able to recognize the possibility that the husband's departure had little to do with her, or even that it took two to tango within the relationship.

One of the reasons why you may attack yourself when something goes wrong and you are criticized is that when you were being raised, your parents may have criticized you in a global fashion. This type of parental criticism is seen in the backgrounds of almost all approval cravers. Rather than correcting the child's behavior, these parents criticize the entire being of the child. They will say, "You are a bad boy," rather than "You should not do *this specific* behavior." I consistently try to teach parents how to catch a child being good. When a parent recognizes that a child is engaging in a new, positive behavior, especially when it's in an area in which you've previously had to punish him, the parent should call the new, positive behavior to the child's attention.

In each of the case histories we've cited, the women rated *themselves*, their *entire beings*. Albert Ellis states in his book *Humanistic Psychotherapy*:

> If you want a preferable solution to the problem of human worth—and I strongly suggest that you strive for this solution—then you better avoid rating yourself at all. You are not *good* and you are not *bad*—you are merely *you*. You possess many traits, most of which you may (and often would better) rate: your abilities to read, to write, to talk, to run, to jump, to drive, just to name a few. But you never have to jump, as if by

magic, from rating these traits to rating *you*. You can, if you wish, give your various facets, your characteristics, your talents, a report card; but you better not give *you* a similar report card. Then, minus such a self-rating, and minus playing the ego game and the power struggle of vying for "goodness" with other human beings, you can ask yourself "What do I really want in life?" and can try to find those things and enjoy them.

## Gods and Devils

The "I am great and you aren't, and the world will correctly honor me and damn you" game played by approval cravers almost invariably accompanies this overrating of self. Again, this game is entirely based on how you do versus how I'm doing. So, if I do well, I am deified. If I do poorly, I am vilified. If you do well, I am vilified. If you do poorly, I am deified.

Ellis goes on to say:

> There really is no answer to the question "What am I worth?" or "How do I prove I am a good person?" since the question is rather meaningless and foolish in the first place. If I ask myself "What do I do?" "What are my traits?" or "What is the value of a performance of mine?" such a question is meaningful since it inquires about a trait, characteristic, or performance which (1) can be observed, and (2) can to some degree be measured or rated. Thus, I play tennis, I possess a good backhand swing in this game, and my particular performance at tennis today was good since I won all the matches I engaged in with competitors. But if I ask myself, "Who am I?," how am I going to answer this question *except* in the light of my traits, characteristics, and performances. How am I to give a meaningful answer to such a vague, undefinable, rather meaningless question?

The key to overcoming these pointless self-rating games and comparisons is for you to avoid rating or evaluating yourself at all. It makes sense for the approval craver to conclude that "I am going to live my life and give myself pleasure on the basis of the idea that it is good for me to live and to enjoy myself." If you decide on that basis, you avoid rating or evaluating yourself completely, although you do evaluate your performances. That is living and enjoying. Without any self-evaluation, without any report carding, you can make the decision to continue to live and have as much enjoyment in life as you can find. Therefore, your major questions to yourself do not become "Who am I?," "Who am I without that man's approval?," "What is my identity without that guy loving me?," or "What is my worth if things don't go well?" The correct questions should become "What are my traits?" "What are my talents?" "What sorts of things do I enjoy and not enjoy doing, and how can I improve my talents and traits?" and "How can I modify my liabilities so that I can continue to live and have a reasonably satisfying existence?"

The point of the cartoon on the next page is that you can't make any judgment about eye color, for example, being worth more than a tennis game, or desirability to spouse more important than education. We are not the sum of our parts, and it is therefore very difficult to determine what each of our traits weighs. Therefore, let's dispense with self-rating entirely. We never rate self, we only rate what we do, our performances. When the women described above fell apart because a man criticized their performance, they were devastated not because their performance was less than perfect, but because they had made a general, irrational assumption that their entire beings were being devalued. They concluded that their essential selves were worthless.

Justine, for example, would come to therapy sessions after a particularly difficult time with her hypercritical and somewhat abusive husband, and tell me, "I came home late again and he blasted me. He called me a slut and a whore; then he started to cry and asked me why I hurt him this way."

Dr. Lubetkin: "How did you feel before, during, and after this incident occurred?" (It's very important that I get a feel for exactly what was going on.)

J.: "Well, before, I felt fine. I was having a good day. During his assault on me, I went into my typical numb shock. I couldn't believe what was happening to me. I felt dazed, dreamlike. I kind

# Which of these characteristics represents your true self?

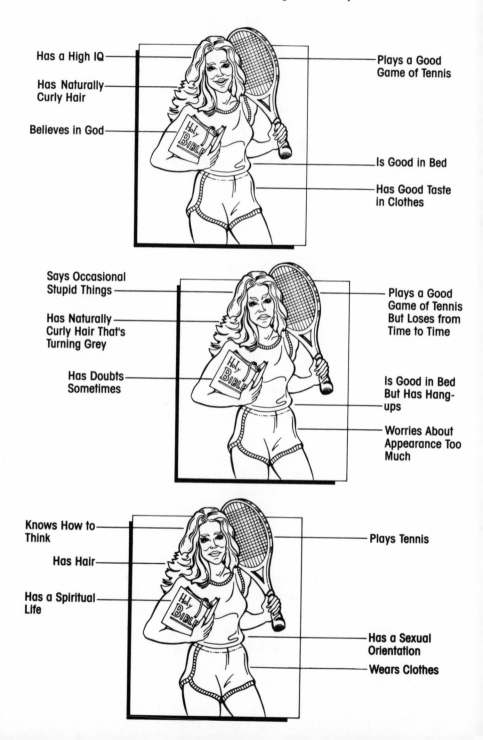

Has a High IQ

Has Naturally Curly Hair

Believes in God

Plays a Good Game of Tennis

Is Good in Bed

Has Good Taste in Clothes

Says Occasional Stupid Things

Has Naturally Curly Hair That's Turning Grey

Has Doubts Sometimes

Plays a Good Game of Tennis But Loses from Time to Time

Is Good in Bed But Has Hang-ups

Worries About Appearance Too Much

Knows How to Think

Has Hair

Has a Spiritual Life

Plays Tennis

Has a Sexual Orientation

Wears Clothes

of detached from the whole experience. I guess that's the way I handle anxiety and abuse. After the incident, I guess I did what you cautioned me not to do, Dr. Lubetkin. I started downing myself; I felt miserable and depressed."

Dr. Lubetkin: "Yes, you took out your report card once again, Justine, and you gave yourself an F. First of all, let's remember that you had the right to stay out. You are an adult and you have the right to come home whenever you want."

J.: "But look, doctor, if the truth be told, I think I was punishing him for being so mean to me. I think I stayed out purposely late, what you call passive-aggressive, doc. Doesn't that make me bad?"

Dr. Lubetkin: "No. Even if your behavior was mean-spirited or punitive, that simply indicates that when you are pushed you fight back in the way you have learned. It may be a style of fighting, Justine, that you don't like or admire about yourself, and I recognize that it may not be the best style of fighting. Clearly there may be better ways we can discuss. Or you may wish you could stop that style of fighting, but it surely says nothing significant about your whole being. You apparently made yourself feel miserable because you devalued your entire being, agreeing with his assessment of your worthlessness. You would not have felt nearly as bad if you had stopped devaluing yourself and believing that you should be temporarily or eternally damned and punished. Instead, you needed to realize that you as a human being are not ratable in any way. Your deeds may be ratable, but your humanness, your essence, is not. Each time in the future that you feel like a rat, Justine, you had better vigorously make yourself realize that you are rating yourself negatively and decide to challenge and correct this self-rating. You must, you will, unconditionally accept yourself although you may forever continue to be troubled by and prefer not to accept a great deal of your behavior, including your punitive, passive-aggressive style. You will correctly keep rating and evaluating your traits, but you will never rate *you*."

Abraham Maslow provides a wonderful description of people who have achieved self-acceptance, as quoted in *The Principles and Practice of Rational-Emotive Therapy* by Wessler and Wessler:

They can accept their own nature in stoic style, with all its shortcomings, with all its discrepancies from the ideal image, without feeling real concern. It would convey the wrong impression to say that they are self-satisfied. What we must say is that they can take the frailties and sins, weaknesses and evils of human nature in the same unquestioning spirit with which one accepts the characteristics of nature. One does not complain about water because it is wet, or about rocks because they are hard, or about trees because they are green. As the child looks out upon the world with wide, uncritical eyes, simply noting and observing what is the case, without either arguing the matter or demanding that it be otherwise, so does the self-actualizing person tend to look upon human nature in himself and in others. This is of course not the same thing as resignation in the Eastern sense, but resignation too can be observed in our subjects, especially in the face of illness and death.

Here let's do an exercise called self-acceptance imagery. Find a quiet place and relax yourself thoroughly. Imagine yourself in a similar situation to that experienced by Justine or any of the women we've described earlier in this chapter. You can read over your record of incidents and find an event that actually occurred in which you were criticized mightily. You are being criticized by someone, preferably by someone with whom you are close.

Recreate that situation in your mind as best you can. You are going to change your thinking so that you are able to feel that a trait is being criticized but *your being* is not. Do whatever you can in your mind to move from a feeling of being decimated to a feeling of being somewhat annoyed and determined to improve the trait.

Record on a piece of paper how you were able in your own, individual way to change your feelings from being decimated to having just the trait criticized and making a decision, if you wish, to improve that particular trait without feeling that your entire being was trampled on.

Write down the types of thoughts you used to make that

cognitive switch based on the philosophic ideas you've read in this chapter. Suggested thoughts you might use could be, "It may be true that I'm not neat and a great homemaker, but that's just one, small part of who I am. Basically I have chosen to accept myself and not to rate my being." Another thought might be, "I am working on becoming a better parent. I lacked good parenting as a child and therefore I did not have effective models, but I'm working on it. Parenting is certainly not my entire being, not everything that matters. It is a trait that I am trying to maximize and improve. Parenting has nothing to do with my essence, which I am choosing to accept without rating."

What I often tell my patients is that "I am not a psychotherapist. I am a person who practices psychotherapy from 8 AM to 7 PM. Suppose I'm thrown out of psychology and I'm looking around for another job, a new way of creating income. I may study, take exams, and become a stockbroker, something I've been interested in all my life."

My client may say to me: "Now you have less income, less prestige, less power. You probably move from your co-op to a less expensive neighborhood, remove your children from private school. Your whole life is diminished in many ways."

Dr. Lubetkin: "But it's quite conceivable that I will continue to be reasonably happy and relatively fulfilled in my life despite having adopted a very different lifestyle. I still have the same traits, qualities, and loyalties. I'm still the same husband, father, and friend."

Client: "People might turn away from you."

Dr. Lubetkin: "Then I would meet new people. And, anyway, my friends receive more from me than what is based on who I am professionally. It's true that some acquaintances are only interested in picking my brain for psychological expertise or get off on the fact that they have a published author to dinner, but it certainly would not be true of most of the people who care about me. Many of them couldn't care less what I do for a living. Our friendship has much more to do with the loyalty, the humor, the history we've created together. Therefore, this would help a great deal to avoid awfulizing or catastrophizing if I had to leave the psychology profession. My occupation is not at the core of my very existence or being. The respect of my friends, the love of my wife and children are not defined by whether or not I am actively practicing psychotherapy."

# STOPPING DISAPPROVAL ANXIETY IN ITS TRACKS THROUGH RELAXATION, DESENSITIZATION, FLOODING, AND VISUALIZATION

♦

By now you realize that much of your fear of disapproval from a significant other is mediated by cognitive distortions (misguided belief systems) or your visceral feelings of fear, or by your lack of appropriate assertive skills.

Nearly all approval cravers are anxious. One of the best ways of treating anxiety is through relaxation skills and other techniques we will introduce in this chapter. However, before we teach you that, we want to help you improve your ability to visualize in that so many of these techniques require good visualization skills. There are several points to recognize when you are practicing the visualizations and imagery in this chapter.

♦ *First, you must identify your major representation system. Every-one has a different representation system, which means what sense you use when you practice visualization. Do you* hear *your mother when you think of her or do you* see *your mother? Do you* smell *the coffee, or do you* hear *the coffee brewing, or do you* see *the coffee, or can you* taste *it? The point is that everyone has a major representational system that they use when they image things in their minds. You can enhance your imagery ability for this chapter by actually exercising that power.*

A good way of exercising and improving your visualization abilities is to imagine some household objects or situations that are benign and non–anxiety-producing, such as the toaster, the iron, your bed, or your room. Just observe how you imagine them. Is it strictly visual, as most people experience, or are other systems working?

Take me on a tour of your home, through each room. Are we hearing things, smelling things, seeing things, feeling things, or even tasting things?

♦ *Another important aspect in visualization is to view the image from the inside out, rather than from the outside. Imagine you are on a roller coaster at the highest point on the track, about to descend. Now it's careening toward the bottom and people behind you are screaming and yelling. Are you seeing that roller coaster scene from the front seat, feeling the wind blowing against your face, your mouth wide open, the ground rushing up to you quickly, or are you standing on the ground, watching yourself in the roller coaster from that faraway vantage point? In the following exercises we want you to see yourself as if you're in the front seat.*

Another way to figure that out is to close your eyes and imagine a clock is on your forehead and the clock is reading 3:00. Is the little hand pointing to the left or to the right? If it's pointing to the right, you are outside, facing yourself. If it's pointing to the left, you are viewing the clock from the inside out.

## Relaxation Exercises

You can accept and incorporate alternative beliefs much more clearly when you are relaxed. You are more open to "reprogramming," for taking in suggestions of new patterns of thought and behavior that will eventually replace the old, worn-out, depressing, negative patterns. Fear and depression are often experienced as so horrendous and distracting that it feels impossible to attend to and integrate new, healthier thoughts and to attempt new, corrective behaviors.

Research has shown that in order for deep relaxation or meditation to be effective, you must have at least one period of relaxation daily, lasting a minimum of fifteen to twenty minutes. Training begins with focusing on breathing and muscle relaxation and then moves on to focusing on letting go rather than harboring any thoughts that come in. It does not matter what form of relaxation you employ. What matters is that you have a consistent and deep experience of relaxation. In such a state, thoughts occur less frequently and do not become fixations. Your breathing becomes slow and regular, and muscles are experienced as deeply relaxed. This state might be characterized by a heavy, weighty sense of your body, or the opposite—you may feel a light, floating sensation. People often report feeling quiet, focused, and passive. All of these sensations are usually indications of being deeply relaxed.

The following is only one of the many techniques that can bring you to this desired state of deep relaxation. It is important that you understand a relaxation period means time alone in a quiet environment in which you will not be disturbed, even by the telephone or doorbell. It does not mean lying back on the sofa with your feet up, gazing at the tube, a can of beer in your hand. During deep relaxation, you are to refrain from any other activity. You can record the instructions for any of the following techniques so that you can follow the procedure, guided by your own voice.

## Contraction Release or Progressive Relaxation

One of the commonest methods of relaxation is based on the principle of contraction release, in which you tense successive muscle groups of your body and then let go. As you tense a group of muscles, hold them as tightly as possible; then let go and relax completely. Best results are gained through regular practice.

Begin by arranging your body in a comfortable, receptive position. Lying on your back on the floor is preferable, but you may sit in a chair if you wish. Uncross your legs and extend your arms, palms facing up. Take three long, full breaths, exhaling completely with each breath. Feel your body letting go of tension with each exhalation.

Clench your right fist and hold the tension there, tighter and tighter. Study the tension in your right fist as you keep the rest of your body relaxed. Then drop the tension in your right fist and allow the sensation of relaxation to flow in. Observe the difference between relaxation and tension as a pleasant, heavy feeling of relaxation floods your hand—into your palm, into each finger. Now clench your left fist and then release the tension in the same manner.

Clench both fists and straighten both arms, tensing the muscles in both arms. Hold the tension. Observe the tension. Now release the tension in both arms and let them drop to your sides. Observe the warm, heavy feeling of relaxation flowing into your arms, down the elbows, through the wrists, into the palms. Feel yourself letting go, relaxing. Take a long, deep breath. Exhale slowly, becoming even more relaxed.

Take another long, deep breath, filling your lungs. Hold the air in your chest, observing the tension created. Now exhale slowly, observing the walls of your chest loosen as the air is pushed out. Continue relaxing and breathing freely and gently.

Tighten your abdominal muscles by pushing them up and out as far as they can go. Hold the tension there and study it. Release the abdominal muscles and allow the feeling of relaxation to flow into each muscle. Continue breathing freely and easily. Each time you exhale, notice the pleasant sensation of relaxation spreading throughout your body.

Tense your buttocks and thighs by pressing down as hard as you can and by pinching your buttocks muscles together. Hold the tension and study it. Release and allow a deep, soothing feeling of relaxation to flow in.

Tense your lower legs by pressing both feet down and pointing your toes. Hold the tension in your legs and feet. Release the tension and allow rejuvenating relaxation to flow in. Breath in and out easily and allow relaxation to flow throughout your body.

Tense your back and shoulders by pinching your shoulders together and arching your back off the floor. Hold the tension and then let go, allowing your back to drop to the floor and feeling relaxation spread. Roll your head back and forth very gently from side to side, releasing the muscles in the back of your neck.

Tense your facial muscles by sticking out your tongue as far as it will go, closing your eyes tightly and wrinkling up your forehead. Hold the tension, then release, allowing warm relaxation to flow through the scalp, forehead, eyelids, cheeks, jaw, even the tongue.

Now allow your body to experience heaviness, as if it were boneless and only the floor is keeping you from sinking. You may, at this time, make a mental inventory of the parts of your body you have contracted and released, telling yourself as you go through your body that each part is heavy, warm, and relaxed, thereby allowing your relaxation to go even deeper.

When you are ready to enter the waking state, begin by gently wiggling toes and fingers, gradually moving into whatever larger stretches your body seems to want. Roll to one side in a fetal position, place one palm on the ground, and push off to lift your body into a sitting position.

## Diaphragmatic Breathing

This is an important technique because many people tense up in situations in which either assertiveness is an issue or they feel attacked or criticized or crave approval. Very often, they will hyperventilate and disrupt the balance between oxygen and carbon dioxide in their blood, becoming light-headed, experiencing anxiety and rapid heartbeat, and generally feeling uncomfortable. This quick and easy technique ensures that you will breathe naturally.

1. Relax your entire body as completely as you can.
2. Breathe in through your nose in a natural, gentle way.
3. Allow the breath to travel all the way to the bottom of your belly, to the diaphragm. Gently *expand* your belly to take in each breath. Keep your shoulders and chest as still as possible. (It might help you to put one hand on your chest and one hand on your stomach in order to monitor the movement in your chest and stomach. The goal is to keep the stomach moving up and down and the chest as still as possible.)
4. Breathe out *slowly* through your mouth, emptying the belly and relaxing the jaw, letting it drop. Breath out as slowly as you can, making each exhale last. Do not hold your breath between inhalations and exhalations.
5. Be sure to breathe in a slow, gentle, and natural manner. Do not hyperventilate (rapid breathing that leads to dizziness or light-headedness).

## Sensory Awareness

This technique begins in the following way. You tell yourself, "I am going to try a series of experiments with myself; each experiment is in the form of a question and each question is answerable by saying either yes or no to myself."

All you have to do is, as you imagine each image, answer yes or no as to whether or not you are able to imagine it successfully. Pause for at least five seconds before imagining each of the following scenarios:

- Is it possible for you to feel the slightest breeze blowing across your face?

- Is it possible for you to become aware of whether or not one arm feels heavier than the other?
- Is it possible for you to be aware of the point of maximum contact between your back and the chair?
- Is it possible for you to become aware of the space within your mouth?
- Is it possible for you to imagine a beautiful flower suspended just a few feet in front of you? What color is it?
- Is is possible for you to just drift along lazily?
- Is it possible for you to feel like a rag doll, floppy and heavy?
- Is it possible for you to imagine yourself floating on a white, fluffy cloud, carefree and relaxed?
- Is it possible for you to imagine whether or not one leg feels warmer or heavier than the other?
- Is it possible for you to imagine something very pleasant?
- Is it possible for you to now imagine a very beautiful sunset?

This technique has been proven effective in reducing cognitive anxiety—that is, mental anxiety. We experience physical tension in our musculature and mental tension in our minds. The first two techniques, progressive relaxation and breathing, are designed to calm down your muscles and viscera. This technique is designed to calm down your thinking and your mind.

## Instruction for Use of Relaxation Techniques

The following progress chart and instructions have been adapted from instructions developed by Dr. Steven T. Fishman of the Institute for Behavior Therapy.

### 1. Formal Training Period (Weeks 1–3)

Practice your chosen method of deep relaxation at least once a day. Practice at a time when you are not overly tired and when distractions can be minimized. Dim the lights and lie on a sofa, bed, or floor. The goal is not to fall asleep but to get in touch with feelings and sensations that accompany relaxation. Do not actively attempt to make use of the relaxation in any way during this period.

### 2. *Phasing Period (Week 4)*

During this period, practice step 1 every other night of the week. On the "off" night, lie on the same sofa, bed, or floor you have been using for your training using the same environmental conditions, but for a period of time not to exceed ten minutes. During this time, attempt to relax yourself by the use of cue words such as calm, heavy, relaxed, or by the use of some previously decided emotive imagery. You might imagine a particularly pleasant scene out of nature or any image that connotes relaxation to you.

### 3. *Incorporate Period (Week 5)*

During this period, use the relaxation procedure you have been following, but only two times. On all other nights, practice merely using the cue words and/or emotive imagery for a period not to exceed ten minutes. More important, however, is that during this period you will begin to use these same cue words or images as you go through your everyday routines, so that relaxation can begin to be incorporated into your normal functioning. You can take fifteen to thirty seconds out of each hour, if possible, to close your eyes and subvocally utter the cue words regardless of your level of activity at the time.

### 4. *Discretionary Period (Week 6 and Thereafter)*

Use the relaxation procedure at your discretion. Do not use it too often because for the relaxation training to be successful, the skill of relaxing must become yours rather than dependent on whichever of the formal relaxation procedures you chose to follow. You are urged to continue using the cue words as you go through your everyday routines and to be consciously aware of relaxing any and all muscle groups that are not being actively used for a specific task. Practice relaxing in a variety of situations and circumstances, such as in the shower, while sitting on public transportation, in a standing position, and so on.

## Affirmative Visualizations

You are able to focus on the following approval-craving issues more clearly in a relaxed state than when you are in a deep state of hypervigilance. Relaxation is perfectly safe; you can make a tape of your own words and play it for yourself. Even if you are skeptical, all evidence seems to indicate that it will work to increase your ability to resist your approval-craving tendencies.

These visualizations are particularly important because the approval craver is constantly creating negative, self-downing images in her mind. Imagine your mind as a movie screen. As you go through life craving approval and fearing disapproval, you keep playing the same movie over and over in your head. This technique will help you change the movie. The following is a useful exercise involving visualization, to be done after you are relaxed.

## Observation and Correction

1. Close your eyes and imagine a situation in which you are unassertive and working hard for approval. Look at your diary for real-life examples.

2. Check your body language in your imagery: your eye contact, posture, the position of your arms. Is your position nondefensive?

3. Observe your struggle to assert yourself and overcome your tendency to want the person's approval.

4. See yourself succeeding. These last steps are extremely important because we want to teach you to cope, rather than to master. All approval cravers will have difficulty asserting themselves, seeing themselves as effective, and resisting the tendency to become depressed if they are criticized. We want you, therefore, to see yourself struggling a bit instead of automatically mastering the situation.

5. See yourself liking yourself more; smile to yourself as you see the situation swing in your favor. See yourself enjoying your own personal sense of power and worrying less abut what others think of you.

6. State an affirmation, make a strong upbeat statement that feels already true within this situation. Examples: "I am unconcerned about the other person's approval." "I like myself just the way I am." "I accept myself fully and completely simply because I exist, not because I do anything very well." "I discount the other person's criticism and I choose to love and support myself." These affirmations may seem a bit corny, but repeating them over and over can be very useful in controlling approval craving.

## Systematic Desensitization

The key concept of systematic desensitization is what we call slow, successive approximations (slowly, step by step). First, you *visualize* increasingly severe experiences that provoke approval craving. As you hold these images in your mind, you feed yourself coping self-statements. You are extending the time in which you are subjected to criticism, for example, and you are recognizing that you don't have to feel decimated. It's manageable, it's doable, and you can control the emotions you anticipated would overwhelm you. When you are able to reassure yourself with these statements, you actually practice these exercises in real life, using the same coping self-statements when needed in order to reassure yourself. The key to this technique is to use anxiety as a prompt—a signal to relax—as a signal to cope.

Systematic desensitization has three components. The first is getting as relaxed as possible and calling up relaxation on demand, as you have learned.

The second is setting up a hierarchy of items in which you rank and order your level of approval craving provoked by various scenes, from those that produce the least approval craving to the most approval craving. Be particularly careful to identify those aspects of the situation that are likely to cause you anxiety and those aspects that are likely to be irrelevant. Be aware that what provokes approval craving for one person may not for another, and vice versa, so do not attempt to find some arbitrary means of measuring how much approval craving is *supposed* to be produced by an item. Your own level of approval craving is all that matters. You must draw up an individual hierarchy that is sensitive to your *particular* pattern of approval craving.

Third, while you are in a state of deep relaxation, listen to your tape-recorded hierarchy, and expose yourself visually to these various approval-craving images in order of ascending anxiety, based on what we call the subjective units of disturbance scale (SUDS). The laws of learning indicate that as you expose yourself to a high anxiety situation while in a relaxed state and, at the same time provide yourself with coping self-statements, you greatly reduce the impact of the anxiety by substituting the more adaptive habit (relaxation).

For example, a simple phobia might be a fear of dogs. Depending on the various idiosyncratic anxiety cues—that is, what exactly about dogs produces fear—the person will imagine various scenes involving dogs and rank them in order of least to most anxiety-producing. If three separate anxiety cues operate within this phobia—the size of the dog, whether the dog is free or on a leash, and the distance of the dog from him—the first item in the hierarchy might be, "I see a small poodle two blocks away on a leash." The second item might be, "I see that poodle one block away, and the owner is leaning over to unhook the leash." The third item might be, "I see a German Shepard two blocks away." The fourth item might be, "I see the poodle running loose and coming quite close to me." The fifth item might be, "I see the poodle jumping on my legs." The sixth item might be, "I see the poodle licking my hand." The seventh item might be, "The German Shepard is running loose near me." The person imagines each of these scenes while in a state of relaxation and feeds himself coping self-statements whenever he experiences fear.

Draw up a list of all the various anxiety-producing stimuli

associated with approval craving, as well as coping thoughts you may use to reduce the anxiety associated with these items. Some of these items will produce low-level anxiety and others high-level. The following table provides examples. The first item is rated 1–3; the second item is rated 4–6; the third item is rated 7–9; the fourth item is rated 10.

| SUDS | VIZUALIZED ITEM IN HIERARCHY | SAMPLE COPING STATEMENT |
|------|------------------------------|-------------------------|
| 1–3 | A friend tells me she heard that my boyfriend used to dump girls if they weren't compliant. I feel tense. | "This is just hearsay, and if he's that superficial, is he really in my best interest? If he disappears, I will survive." |
| 4–6 | My boyfriend tells me that I'm selfish if I skip his party to go out with the girls. I feel unsure of myself and worried. | "Stop awfulizing. A relationship is a series of compromises, and he must learn to do this, too. It's highly unlikely this will escalate, and, if it does, I will survive." |
| 7–9 | My lover informs me that he found another woman at a party sexually attractive. I panic. | "Where is it written that he should never find anyone else attractive? Why am I continually assuming it means I'm unattractive? Relax. Don't get defensive. I don't need 100 percent of his attention 100 percent of the time. Every other indication says that I can trust him." |

| 10 | My lover in a drunken stupor tells me to "get out of his life." I'm terrified. What will I do? | "Calm and steady. By allowing his drinking problem to go untreated, he is not respecting my needs. His disapproval of me is his problem. I have proven I can survive without him." |

Now list the scenes in the table and any others you imagine in hierarchical order, beginning with least to most anxiety-producing. Remember, those scenes you find most anxiety-producing might not affect others as profoundly. Different people have different trigger situations.

How do you know a situation produces anxiety in you? First of all, you know which situations are likely to bother you the most by real-life experiences. If you have avoided certain situations or feel a flood of anxiety when you contemplate those situations, they are clearly anxiety-producing for you. You may look over your list and ask yourself, "Which of these situations has occurred in my life and bothered me the most?"

Another way to determine if a situation is anxiety-producing is to close your eyes and imagine the situation. Tune in closely to how you feel. Is there a quickening in your breathing? Is there an increase in heart rate? Are there knots in your stomach? Are your shoulders tense? Do you feel a tinge of a headache?

After you have set up the hierarchy of scenes, assign each of the items a SUDS rating from 1 to 10, depending on how tense each scene makes you feel. Then, if you wish, tape each one at a time.

Go through the first scene while in a state of deep relaxation. Imagine the item as clearly as you can. See it as if it were happening at this very moment. Hold the scene for at least one minute. Use any anxiety you experience as a signal or prompt to go back into deep relaxation while holding onto the image. Use cue words (such as release or calm) to help. Relax your muscles, deepen your breathing, and calm your mind. Maintain the scene. Now use your anxiety as a means of identifying your self-defeating thoughts. What are you telling yourself that is frightening you? Once you have done that, find a healthy replacement thought. These new cognitions can come from work in Chapter 3 or from any other scene that helps you create corrective thoughts. Relax again, drop the scene for thirty seconds, and then reimagine the scene. Repeat the process as long as necessary. Once you are able to expose yourself to the scene three consecutive times for about one minute each without experiencing anxiety, you have met the desensitization criteria and can move on to the next scene in your hierarchy.

## *Flooding*

Another helpful technique for dealing with approval craving is to imagine yourself in the highest anxiety-provoking situation possible. Stay with it until the anxiety is extinguished. Here, relaxation and coping thoughts are *not* used. Mere exposure to the feared disapproval situation will ultimately lead to it's not eliciting as much fear. If someone who is fearful is kept in the provoking situation long enough, the anxiety eventually dissipates. For example, if someone is afraid of dogs and is placed in a room with dogs without permission to leave, after going through hell for a while, the anxiety will eventually dissipate. Flooding approval needs works exactly the same way.

Imagine a situation in which you have experienced your greatest humiliation, as far as approval craving is concerned. Consult your diary for appropriate circumstances, or you might imagine yourself at a nightclub or a bar. You are interested in a man who turns away from you to talk to another pretty woman. They are smiling in your direction, as if they are making fun of you. Hold that scene. Stay with that image and make it even worse. Blow it up. Now they're pointing in your direction and laughing to each other. You are convinced they are laughing about you. Stay with the scene, even if you have to do so for an hour or more. Stay with it until the anxiety and uncomfortable feelings dissipate. It will always go away because it is not reinforced.

Anytime you feel anxiety about something and you expose yourself to the situation and nothing terrible actually happens—that is, your worst fears are not realized—eventually the anxiety goes away. The body cannot stay anxious forever; physiologically and psychologically you tire of the anxiety. Finally, you expose yourself to the scene and feel no anxiety at all.

Another scene might involve you at a party at which no one talks to you. In fact, they are even moving away from you. Or your lover comes in one morning, takes one look at your morning face and says, "Ugh, you look disgusting without makeup!" Hold that scene, hear his remark, and hold that sound and image until you no longer feel upset by it.

# RISK-TAKING AND SHAME ATTACK EXERCISES THAT WILL RID YOU OF SHAME AND EMBARRASSMENT ONCE AND FOR ALL

♦

With risk-taking exercises, you are asked to risk whatever you fear; in this case, disapproval and rejection. Risk means the possibility of an unpleasant outcome, the probability of which cannot be predicted. The outcome might be 0 percent unpleasant to 100 percent unpleasant. But you must learn to take the risk, to see what happens.

Shame attack exercises, originally developed by Dr. Albert Ellis, differ from risk-taking exercises in several respects. First, there's a much higher possibility of rejection or disapproval associated with shame attacks. Second, you are learning to overcome the emotion that inhibits you from taking the risk. In other words, you are dealing with the fear of feeling shame—a fear of feeling disapproved of or disagreed with—as opposed to the risk-taking exercises in which you are really just practicing taking the risk. The third difference is that shame attack exercises are activities we would never really spontaneously engage in on our own.

Risk-taking and shame attack help you overcome your fear of disapproval. The following is a list of risk-taking exercises taken from the most recent group of activities I gave to patients to help them overcome the fear of disapproval, the major underlying fear for approval cravers.

## Risk-Taking Exercises

♦ *Smile at five strangers.*

Pamela was always uncomfortable with the disapproval of strangers and was convinced that people would always be unpleasant to her. This assignment helped her realize that at least 50 percent of the time people smiled back.

♦ *Ask for directions to find a particular product at the supermarket and then extend the conversation.*

Lucy was convinced that if she bothered people with the burden of her conversation, she would be rejected. All of her conversations were questions and answers; if she chatted with people, they would be sure to move on. Lucy discovered from her assignment that people didn't run away from her and that many did want to talk.

♦ *Stop people on the street who appear to be in a hurry, and ask them where the post office is.*

Again, this is for people who are concerned about being intrusive and are overconcerned with people's movements. Deedee came to see me complaining about fear of intruding on the time of others. She had always been taught to defer to authority or to people who appeared to be in a hurry. After performing the exercise, she realized that many people who appear to be in a hurry are actually not, and are willing to stop to give directions. As with many of these exercises, she felt empowered.

♦ *Ask your boss for a raise.*

With any of these exercises, of course, you must be sure the consequences will not be dangerous for you. If you are sure that not only will the boss turn you down but fire you, don't do this exercise. But this is endemic for those afraid of asking for a raise and for appreciation of merit.

Sunny kept obsessing for weeks about asking her boss for a raise. When she finally got up the nerve, even though she didn't receive the raise, he was responsive to her. Again, the issue in many of these risk-taking exercises is not that the outcome will be exactly what you wanted, but that you are empowering yourself. People are reckoning with you.

♦ *Rent an adult movie.*

This is a particularly good exercise for an individual who is concerned that he might be disapproved of by strangers for his taste, or for somebody who thinks there might be something wrong with him. This is a particularly good exercise for people such as Caitlin, who was overconcerned about people's possible disapproval of her taste. Caitlin had long wondered about the nature of these adult movies. On a few occasions, her boyfriends had offered to show her, but she'd always demurred and turned them down. She was also extremely curious about sexual experimentation, although she had no one to really guide her. She and I agreed that asking for an adult movie in her local video store would be difficult, but it would empower her to recognize that she had the right; she was an adult, this was nothing to be ashamed of, and millions of people around the country were doing this every day. It was highly unlikely that the people behind the counter would sit in negative judgment of her. If they did, it was their problem.

♦ *Go to a movie alone.*

Many people view this as a major risk. They don't want to be seen alone on Saturday night. They have this wild idea that everyone at the theater will be in couples and view them as weird.

Gladys was requested by me to actually count the number of other single people in the lobby at the theater, and to count them again when everyone sat down. She discovered that approximately one-third of the people in the movie theater were by themselves. This directly conflicted with the prediction I'd asked her to make earlier when she was convinced she'd be the only single person in the theater. The act empowered her with new information and new courage.

♦ *Call a taxicab and then change your mind after the taxicab pulls up.*

Once they commit to a decision, many approval cravers don't feel free to change their minds for fear of upsetting the other person. Rosemarie, a twenty-nine-year-old secretary, was terrified of upsetting people if she should change her mind. Often, she'd find herself making a decision—for example, about going to a show or a restaurant—that she would regret but felt she couldn't back out of for fear of upsetting the other person. The taxicab exercise was perfect for her, as were the following two exercises, all of which Rosemarie accomplished. These were all about getting additional information and changing her mind. Rosemarie became much more effective and empowered on her job and more willing to make decisions in her social life after she had undergone a number of these risk-taking situations.

♦ *Call the information operator and ask for the address rather than the phone number.*

Some people live their lives playing strictly by the rules, and are intimidated from varying even to the slightest extent.

♦ *Ask for change of a quarter on the street and then change your mind and ask for your quarter back.*

Some approval cravers will get a ticket on their car because they didn't have change of a dollar for the meter and were reluctant to bother a stranger to give it to them.

♦ *Sit in front of the class and ask questions.*

Many are afraid of calling attention to themselves and being made a fool of. They refuse to sit up front where they might be called on.

Karen, a nineteen-year-old student, would slink to the back of the classroom. I encouraged her to sit up front and to formulate questions and ask them. She was able to do this in successive approximations, at each class moving further and further to the front of the class. She first asked questions that she and a friend agreed would be reasonable, and, after a while, she was able to formulate her own.

♦ *Disagree with someone in class.*

Karen also dared to disagree with another classmate, taking the risk of feeling a bit foolish. By the end of the semester, she felt comfortable performing these types of exercises.

♦ *Ask someone to stop smoking.*

Another student was instructed to ask a peer to stop smoking during class.

♦ *Return an item to a store.*

A woman named Semi was extremely uncomfortable in commercial situations, particularly dealing with clerks and waiters. The next three exercises were accomplished successfully by Semi. She returned an item to a store with a policy of "no returns." Her goal was not necessarily to have them accept it, but to at least argue her case. Again, the emphasis was not necessarily on winning but on having people reckon with her.

♦ *Send back a rare steak and ask that it come back medium or well.*

I accompanied Semi to a restaurant and helped her return an overly rare steak by reminding her that she was the consumer, with the right to have her order the way she wanted it.

♦ *Enter a restaurant and ask to see the health certificate.*

This exercise is helpful for those who are afraid that others will question their motives. This was a particularly effective exercise for Semi, who was afraid people would question her motives and that people in her local coffee shop might think she finds it's too dirty. She was very concerned about offending the owner. I pointed out that it was her right as a consumer to request the health certificate. I modeled the act for her in other restaurants, and nine times out of ten, the owners were a bit intimidated and brought out the certificate. On two occasions, I was even offered a free meal, even though I had never eaten at the restaurant. Again, the point is to feel empowered and in control.

♦ *Ask for change of a dollar from a store without buying anything.*

Tania was asked to carry out this exercise and the following one. She was always concerned about disrupting people, intruding on them, and asking them for favors or requests they might not want to grant. She was sent into a number of stores to ask for change. Some turned her down; many did not. Again, the point was empowerment, to do something that has an uncertain ending.

♦ *Go to the restroom after a movie starts.*

Some people will stay frozen in their seat even though they need to relieve themselves because they are afraid of risking disapproval by disturbing other movie viewers when they pass by.

Tania was also instructed to go to the restroom after the movie had started. Ordinarily, she would sit for the entire movie for fear of upsetting some strangers or having to deal with their "tsks." She became expert in overcoming these fears.

♦ *Leave a small tip when service at a restaurant is mediocre or poor.*

Zena was raised to believe that one always must be proper and do what she defined as the right thing. She never risked doing the wrong thing and therefore lived her entire life on the straight and narrow. Whereas this was fine in many situations, sometimes it left her too vulnerable and overconcerned about what others would think of her. She was encouraged to leave a small tip where the service was poor, where, usually, she would have left 15 percent, no matter what.

♦ *Don't bring a gift to a birthday party for a person you know slightly or not at all.*

This is effective for people like Zena, who live their lives always doing the right thing. While Zena was in therapy with me, she was invited to a party by wealthy people she hardly knew, who would expect an expensive gift she couldn't afford. She was terrified to show up without a gift, fearing that they would censor her in the future. I pointed out that because she had no great interest in developing a relationship with these people, and because she did not want to bring an inexpensive gift—although that would have been the ideal solution—she could bring no gift at all. She did so, and there were no negative consequences.

♦ *Call a doctor you've seen and ask for advice over the phone.*
Zena also did this exercise, and, again, there were no negative consequences.

Choose from the previous exercises or make up your own. Risk-taking exercises will demonstrate to you that (a) you can do it, (b) the sky won't fall down on you, (c) you might get exactly the results you want, (d) your self-esteem is enhanced, and (e) even if the worst happens, it's not as bad as you imagined. Unless you are willing to take these risks and do these exercises, you will get nowhere with overcoming your approval craving. The following are risk-taking exercises specific to relationships with significant others.

♦ *Tell your partner no—about anything. Just stand up to him and say no.*
Stella found it impossible to say no to her partner about anything. Even when she violently disagreed with him, she would couch her objection in all sorts of caveats and excuses. For example, he very much wanted to double-date with a couple whom she strongly disliked. Rather than say no, she made up all sorts of excuses, and when they didn't work, she developed a severe headache the night of the date. We did a good deal of practicing—role playing—getting Stella to say no to minor requests. He would ask her to draw a bath for him, and she would yell out, "No, I can't do that. I'm busy cooking." Gradually, we moved to being able to say no without providing any excuse at all. That was the goal: not to provide any justification, to feel comfortable saying a simple no.

♦ *Suggest something slightly kinky or naughty sexually.*
Stella was also a classic case of someone who had grown up in a restricted, sheltered environment, but harbored a curiosity about sexual experimentation. Typically, she was also fearful of suggesting anything out of the ordinary in bed, because her boyfriend was

rather inhibited himself. I suggested some reading, such as *The Joy of Sex,* by Alex Comfort, to see if there was anything she would like to try, sexually, and then suggest it to him. She was afraid he would disapprove of her—accuse her of being a tramp. Again, role playing and learning to voice her opinions in other spheres helped Stella become more assertive about her sexual desires.

♦ *Question your partner's judgment or opinion.*

Jane would come out of a movie she'd seen with her husband, and even if she had strong opinions about it, she would be reluctant to express them if they conflicted with those of her husband. She didn't want to get into any conflicts, but when she finally did express her opinion, she discovered she could fend very well for herself.

♦ *Wear an outfit your partner doesn't like.*

Elaine finally dared to wear a dress her husband didn't like. She simply explained to him that her taste was different from his, and that his tastes had not always been perfect in all areas and that it was important for her to express her individuality.

♦ *Admit to your partner a personality flaw of yours.*

Lorie would hide and hold back from her partner aspects from her past or of her personality. When she shared with him how she occasionally thinks of stealing money from her employer, Lorie took a risk and learned to live with the possibility of his disapproval.

♦ *Tell your partner you don't like someone he adores, or vice versa—someone he dislikes, you do like.*

Jeanine always found it very difficult to tell her husband that she sometimes didn't like the people he seemed to like a lot. He would take a very strong position, adamant about the wonderful virtues of a particular acquaintance, but Jeanine, though insightful about their character flaws, was reluctant to tell her husband about his misperceptions. She felt free, however, to share her views with friends. We worked on getting Jeanine to directly confront him about recognizing the serious character flaws in some of these friends. In the end, he was quite thankful to Jeanine, because these people did turn out to be untrustworthy.

♦ *Forget to bring him something he has requested of you.*

Yolanda was overly compliant to her partner. He would send her out on a mission and she would do anything to ensure his approval. Yolanda's assignment was to "forget" her boyfriend's popcorn when she went to the refreshment stand at the movie theater. She returned to her seat with her candy bar and soda and dealt with his disapproval.

## Shame Attack Exercises

Remember, shame attack exercises, as Wessler points out in *The Principles and Practices of Rational-Emotive Therapy,* are

> Directed specifically at overcoming the emotion that occurs when others disapprove of us, given the idea that I must be approved in order to be worthwhile. More to the point, the exercises are directed towards overcoming the fear of disapproval. Just as the person with a fear of snakes avoids snakes at all costs, many people avoid actions or appearances they consider shameful. Thus, a person may be socially inhibited because she is afraid of saying the wrong thing. She may be compulsively proper because she fears what others would think. She may even fail to form her own opinions and values because she fears others will not agree.

Assign yourself shame attack exercises the same way you did the risk-taking exercises. You can either assign them to yourself or ask a friend to help work out exercises she feels would be useful to you. The following are exercises I have assigned to various patients.

♦ *Be forceful in a restaurant.*

You are waiting in a restaurant and the maitre d' tells you it will be fifteen minutes or half an hour. Walk over to a table where it appears as if the party is getting ready to leave and say, "Excuse me, will you be ready to leave soon because we're waiting."

After much discussion regarding the rationale for this exercise at some length, Gladys did the exercise despite her discomfort. To her surprise, the people told her they would be leaving in a few minutes; the sky didn't fall down on her, and she felt empowered. She had done something that was extremely uncomfortable, even somewhat rude, without feeling the shame she was accustomed to experiencing.

♦ *Stand on one side of the street curb and have a friend stand on the other, each of you holding one end of an imaginary string.*

Ask people to walk around it or step over it. The point of this exercise is to again recognize that even if people disapprove or laugh or tsk at you, it's like a movie running through your life. You will never see these people again; their opinion doesn't count. Stop exaggerating the specter of people judging you negatively. In fact, you will find that most people will join in with the frivolity and step over the imaginary string or walk around you.

♦ *Call out the stops on the bus.*

This is a very disinhibiting activity. You may be disturbed at the thought of doing it, but you will find out that no one calls the mental hospital. Although some people will look at you as if you are a bit weird, you can always get off at the next stop and never see these people again. Again, this exercise is empowering because you've challenged the rigid notion that you can't break the rules at all, that you have to be approved of by everyone, and that disapproval is the most awful, shameful experience in the world.

♦ *Wear a sign displaying your problems, such as "I am anxious."*

You are calling attention to yourself and disinhibiting your fear of disapproval.

Barbara was a member of one of my social anxiety groups. Above all, she didn't want the group members to know just how anxious she was, even though they were all working on the same problem! She couldn't believe they would be able to accept and like her if they knew the level of fear she experienced. I had her make up a paper sign and wear it to the next group meeting. It read "I am very anxious." Most of the people congratulated her on her bravery to call attention to her problem, stated that they had liked her from the first meeting, and that there was nothing about the anxiety they all shared that offended any of them. By sharing her fears, she risked the worst possible consequences she could have imagined. Nothing terrible happened, so she was able to significantly reduce her fear of social situations.

♦ *Try to sell a tattered book on the street.*

Barbara had great difficulty doing anything that could be viewed as "poor," so she frantically struggled to keep up with the Joneses, trying to impress others by going into debt for clothing and other material objects that would make her look good for others and gain their approval. One of her assignments was to sell an old book. No one bought it, but she stood on the street for over an hour, accompanied by other group members. She discovered that it wasn't that terrible; no one made fun of her or thought she had called attention to herself in a negative and impoverished way. Her worst fears were not realized.

♦ *Wear stockings with runs or clothes that don't match.*

This exercise is very effective for the perfectionistic approval craver. Again, do not do this if it will land you in a serious situation.

Rhonda, a twenty-two-year old, was a perfectionist who craved approval. She was very narcissistic and wanted everyone to think she was special. Always immaculately groomed and well dressed, Rhonda found it immensely difficult to wear mismatched clothes and stockings with runs. After first wearing the clothes in my office, then the waiting room, Rhonda recognized the importance of doing this exercise, and ultimately was able to go to work and on dates in her less than perfect outfit. The exercise disinhibited her from her perfectionism. She learned that people could still like and respect her, and that she had built a false wall of awfulizing about what would happen "if." Nothing happened "if."

♦ *Call out the time in a department store or the floor in an elevator.*

I have practiced this shame attack with patients many times, particularly in elevators. This exercise reinforces the lesson that you are running movies in other people's minds, and that you can do pretty outrageous things in this world. Most of the time, it will pass, it will be forgotten, and nothing terrible will happen to you. I have often taken groups of patients into an elevator in a large department store in New York, called out the time aloud, and had a number of people look at me as if I was quite weird. Then, as I got off the elevator with the group, I would talk out loud about the distorted thoughts that I was having. "People will call the police." "People will know who I am and ruin my practice." The unreasonable ideas we possess keep us inhibited and prevent us from taking positive risks. I challenged the idea that I had to be ashamed of what I did. By speaking aloud about the experience and sharing these distortions with my patients, they, too, were able to take more risks.

♦ *Play a guitar or piano in a music store.*

Maria was terribly concerned about how her boyfriend might react to her upcoming piano concert. Her exercise was to enter a music store, sit down at a piano, and bang out some wrong notes. People noticed her mistakes, and Maria learned to live with it.

♦ *Wear a sign around your neck on the street that says Advice, Five Cents.*

Sylvia was asked for advice fairly regularly, yet always felt extremely gun shy about giving the advice. The wrong word could ruin their life, she feared, and if her advice turned out to be incorrect, the person would sit in negative judgment on her. Some people on the street actually took Sylvia seriously; others played with her. But doing this exercise took the fear to an extreme level and challenged her shame of doing anything.

The essence of the shame attack exercise is to get the reader to confront her fears directly in a guilt-free, courageous fashion. For example, Roslyn was uncomfortable because her boyfriend loved to flirt with strange women—waitresses, sales clerks, and even her sister. Fearful of being accused of possessiveness and possibly driving away her free-spirited lover, Roslyn bit her tongue and suffered pangs of jealousy and inadequacy in silence. She spent a great deal of time criticizing herself for her jealousy and trying to convince herself that she shouldn't have these feelings. The solution to her problem involved achieving two goals. One was the obvious: helping Roslyn assert herself by explaining to her partner her negative feelings about his behavior. The other involved a greater risk, immersing herself in the very things she was most ashamed of: her own feelings of jealousy and inadequacy. We arranged shame attack exercises involving various increasingly self-revealing activities. For example, one of the most extreme involved wearing a button that read "I am a possessive person and proud of it!"

The rationale for shame attack exercises is that if a person does the thing she is most afraid of over and over, she eventually learns that the sky will not fall down upon her. Approval cravers discover that their fears dissipate as disapproval from the love object begins to count less and less.

# How to Help
# Your Child
# Overcome His
# Craving for
# Approval

♦

$F$or many of you this may be the most important chapter in the book. You feel you can cope somehow with your own issues; you can learn or not learn whatever you need from the previous chapters. But your real concern is that you not pass on your problems to your children, essentially to save them from the approval-craving thoughts and behaviors you've had to face all of your life. In addition, it remains an educational truth that sometimes the best learning comes from teaching others. Even if you don't have children, you can still become a good teacher of these methods (and thereby help yourself!) by identifying a friend, neighbor, or relative, and going over some of these exercises with them.

If you have children, this is a crucial chapter, one you will find yourself referring to again and again. Many of the techniques and approaches discussed earlier can undoubtedly be adapted for children, but children also need their own special techniques, which we will review in this chapter. When we speak of children, we mean from the ages of three up through adolescence and the teen years. Obviously, we cannot review all of the techniques available to help these children overcome approval craving at the various developmental levels. Many of the techniques can be adapted by creative parents to the various age levels. Most important, though, is that you follow a number of principles we will discuss in this chapter that can be extracted for use with any age level. The language and level of attention and intervention the parent takes will vary from age level to age level.

What breaks many parents' hearts is to see their children not able to say no, to see their children overly involved with some other child whom they may disapprove of but the child admires desperately. That other child will often influence the approval-craving child to do dangerous or inappropriate things. Most teenage drug users report that they were earlier influenced by another child who seemed to be very popular. In their eagerness to join the "in" group, they went along with the suggestion about using drugs and alcohol. Parents ache inside when they see their child overly influenced, not being able to say no, going along with the crowd, working overly hard, sometimes even making fools of themselves or being overly compliant in order to be accepted and approved of. And as children enter the school system, parents lose more control as the peer group standards and pressures begin to take over more and more in terms of influencing their children.

Some children are particularly vulnerable to this pressure, and these are the children who become young approval cravers. While most of my practice is with adults, parents will frequently discuss the problems of their children with me. Other than discipline, conduct problems, studying and scholastic motivation, this is the most important issue parents present. Their children's self-esteem; how to get their children not to need approval so much from the peer group; and how to help their children be more independent and autonomous beings, not overly reliant on the approval, love, or affection of others are the main themes I hear.

A number of fine books have been written on the subject of helping children to increase their self-esteem and confidence and to overcome approval needs. These books can be valuable resources for you to which you can refer whenever you wish.

- *The Thinking, Feeling, Behaving Series for All Grades* by Ann Vernon (Research Press). Ms. Vernon puts out two volumes for different age levels, as well as an emotional curriculum for adolescence.
- *Anyone Can Have a Happy Child: The Simple Secret of Positive Parenting* by Jacob Azerrad (M. Evans and Co.)
- *Your Child's Self-Esteem* by Dorothy Corkhill Briggs (Double-day/Dalton)
- *The Six Point Plan for Raising Happy, Healthy Children* by John Rosemond (Andrews and McMeel)
- *Children of Fast Track Parents: Raising Self-Sufficient and Confident Children in an Achievement-Oriented World* by Andree Aelion Books (Penguin)
- *How to Raise an Emotionally Healthy, Happy Child* by Albert Ellis, with Sandra Moseley and Janet Wolfe (Wilshire Book Company)

Most communities also have programs designed as "schools" for parents, with psychologists or psychiatrists teaching some of the skills necessary to deal with children's problems at various ages and how to detect developmental roadblocks in children. Numerous other workshops are often conducted in university or college psychology departments. You may contact me or the Association for the Advancement of Behavior Therapy in New York City, 15 West 36th Street, to find out what therapists are available or what children's workshops are running in your particular community.

Overconcern with the approval of others is a common, almost conventional, phenomenon among children, especially adolescents. Parents have a very difficult time convincing their teenage children otherwise, because peer group pressure is so powerful.

Girls and boys want to dress and act just like the crowd in order to assure acceptance. Wanting to be accepted by their peer group becomes a problem, however, when it leads to the following symptoms.

### ◆ *Depression and Anxiety*

Lucie, a thirteen-year-old, was brought in by her mother with complaints of phobic anxiety in the morning before school, feelings of depression and sadness on the way to school, and lack of motivation in school. After a few sessions, it became clear that Lucie had been feeling increasingly excluded by what she considered the "in" group at school because her clothing was considered by them to be cheap and not fashionable. Their teasing increased the pressure Lucie felt to gain their approval and become part of the group. In this case, I interceded with the school psychologist to plan a number of sessions, including not only my patient but other students, in order to help everyone increase their sensitivity to one another and to not exclude friends because of external appearances. Ultimately, however, Lucie found that she functioned better in a school in which all of the children wore the same uniform and no discrimination was possible.

### ◆ *Running with the Wrong Crowd*

Alda, another thirteen-year-old girl, succumbed to peer pressure in her small New York suburb to break curfew and stay out late with her friends. Her excuse to her parents was, "All the kids do it." I counseled Alda's mother to call other mothers in the community whose children were staying out late and to question whether or not these children had permission to do so. As it turned out, of course, Alda's claims were wildly exaggerated, and all of the mothers pooled their efforts to ensure their children came home on time. Once Alda was reassured that if she came home early, she wouldn't be excluded, she was content to be home when her parents required. Peer pressure at this age is often far more powerful than the relatively puny pressure from parents to tow the line.

### ◆ *Drug and Alcohol Use*

Feliz, a sixteen-year-old, was enticed by the "in crowd" to

experiment with marijuana and alcohol at the parties some of the boys had organized. As a new student in school, Feliz desperately wanted to be a part of this group and felt the only way to be accepted was to go along with these pressures. Her parents, rational and psychologically sophisticated people, were able to work along with Feliz and me to convince her that there were other roads to acceptance and that this path could only lead to difficulty. If those other children were true friends, they would not engineer situations that could only land her in trouble. As it turned out, one child in her school was seriously injured in a drug-related accident, and the entire school community brought pressure to bear on the children who were throwing the wild parties.

### ♦ Crime

Sixteen-year-old Mary got into stealing cars because her friends were doing it and she didn't want to be left out. A look at recent newspaper headlines tells us clearly of the shocking criminal behavior girls and boys can engage in because of peer group pressure.

### ♦ Early Sexual Activity

Laura, a fifteen-year-old, was brought by her parents regarding conduct problems. During our discussions, it came out that she was experimenting sexually with a boy much older than she, who was clearly taking advantage of her innocence and naiveté as well as her need for his approval. Her approval needs had gone so far that when this boy told her there was no need for safe sex and proposed intercourse without a condom, she nearly capitulated. Fortunately, her parents interceded, and my work helped Laura recognize that she was devaluing herself by becoming so swept up in feelings for a boy that had little regard for her and her sensitivity. Whereas early sexual experimentation is often the norm among some groups of young teens, it is nearly always motivated and energized to a great degree by a need for acceptance by the peer group. This is even the case with young boys, who frequently enter into sexual activity before they are psychologically and developmentally ready. But they feel so intensely pressured by other boys that to abstain would be a fate worse than death.

### ♦ Shyness

This child is reticent in any gathering of other children. She will hold back, is uncomfortable communicating, feels left out whether or not she is really being left out, and feels inadequate. Very often, this child is a prime candidate for becoming an adult approval craver because it appears that the only way to win affection and approval from others is to go along with their wishes. Shy children, such as fifteen-year-old Laura, tend to spend excessive time with adults and have better communication with those adults than with their peers. Adults often miss the point that these children are approval seekers because they are often very charming and delightful. But Laura was typical in that she was very uncomfortable with her peers and found the safety of an older person much more compelling in terms of a relationship. At day camp or sleep-away camp, counselors are often impressed with the children who spend time with them and speak intelligently and seriously with them, but very often these children are simply avoiding being with their peer group.

### ♦ Suicide

Some youngsters have even committed suicide because they felt rejected by the group. These approval-craving children are often those who go along with certain high-admiration models: bullies, jocks, or, in the case of girls, the prettiest or most popular girl in the peer group. Approval-craving children allow themselves to be taken advantage of, bullied, unduly influenced, or pushed around—almost enslaved at times—in order to achieve the approval and acknowledgment of other children.

An ironic occurrence at the Institute for Behavior Therapy is that a parent will bring in a child for therapy for shyness or unassertiveness because the child is going along with whatever an admired peer wants her to do. When I interview the parent, it becomes quite clear that the parent has spent her life behaving in a similar way. These are often parents who come in loaded down with the latest designer labels, name-dropping, and otherwise evidencing extreme concern with their appearance. These are the very parents who can't quite understand how their child has picked up this overconcern about image and approval of others. The first step in such cases is to show the parent how she will have to modify some of her behavior and take another look at her values, which the child is naturally picking up.

Thirteen-year-old Chloe was brought in by her mother, who had been separated from Chloe's father for two years. Andrea complained that Chloe was overattached to some classmate of whom Andrea didn't approve. It turned out that Chloe's mother was extremely influenced by people in her own peer group and had been involved with a party crowd from whom she very much wanted approval, even though it was hindering her career aspirations. We had to work with Andrea first to recognize that her best interests were not being served by her crowd, before she could begin to communicate more credible information to Chloe about being independent, self-sufficient, and not needing the approval of others.

The habits, attitudes, and beliefs associated with approval craving begin early in a child's life. The earlier they are caught and modified, the more comfortable the child will be in the adult arena. Various researchers have suggested that there are various family constellations that may produce high-risk-taking children versus those who are overly shy and lacking in self-esteem. Other researchers have suggested birth order is more significant, and still others believe that self-esteem is associated with early parental relationships, particularly if one parent is absent a good deal. Other theorists believe self-esteem is a matter of the temperament with which one is born. Despite all of these theories, what seems to be a constant in all of the children who come to the Institute with approval-craving problems is that the child has learned the following two beliefs.

The first is that approval and acceptance is all-important from others. They try to get *everyone* to believe that they are special and what they do is special, and they work overtime to be admired and liked. The second is that disapproval is devastating. At all costs, they must avoid activities or situations that will cause others to dislike them. They work hard to avoid criticism, risk-taking, and controversy, and they truly believe that it would be terrible if they were disapproved of by others.

As we've noted in other chapters, approval-craving problems cannot be separated from assertiveness problems. There are six dominant reasons why all people, including children, act unassertively. In their landmark book, *Responsible Assertive Behavior: Cognitive Behavioral Procedures for Trainers*, Lang and Jacobowski describe these six major reasons why individuals develop nonassertive behavior.

1. Mistaking firm assertion for aggression. Many individuals' firm assertion sounds like aggression. Thus, people sometimes mislabel their own natural assertive impulses as potentially troublesome urges that must be severely controlled. Little girls, in particular, are socialized to believe this.

Claire, a nine-year-old who was often picked on at school, was brought to me by her parents. It became apparent to me that Claire had never been taught that little girls can express anger or can talk back. If anything, she had been reinforced for being passive, fearful, and compliant. I worked with Claire to help her learn that she had the skills and the right to express her anger, even to her parents, who had never reinforced her ability to express her anger toward them.

2. Learning to mistake nonassertiveness for politeness. Lang and Jacobowski point out that some people act nonassertively under the mistaken notion that this behavior is just being polite and considerate. This was a similar message given to Claire.

3. Failure to accept personal rights, believing that they do not have the right to express their reaction, to stand up for themselves, or to protect their own emotional wants or desires. Often such people don't believe they can legitimately express certain "negative" feelings, such as anger or affection toward others.

Sally, a young girl of eleven, was brought in to see me by her mother because she was acting depressed, not doing well in school, and generally behaving fearfully in a number of situations. It became clear that Sally had never learned she had the right to express anger and disappointment, particularly toward her parents concerning sibling issues. When I gave Sally permission to express these feelings, much of her depression seemed to lift and her confidence and self-esteem improved greatly.

4. Concern or anxiety about the consequences of expressing assertive behaviors or feelings. The general fear is that they will lose other people's love or approval, that others will think they are foolish or self-centered, or that others will feel hurt or damaged by their assertiveness.

Twelve-year-old Stephen was brought in by his parents for problems of being picked on in school and generally not feeling very confident or assertive with his peers. He had been raised by parents who, while very gracious, human, and civil people, had never really discussed with their boy his right to express his feelings of anger and disappointment with others, or assured him that it was highly unlikely that if he did express these feelings, it would result in any long-term negative consequences for others. And even if it did, Stephen needed to learn that he had that right. He had to get others to reckon with him instead of constantly reckoning with their needs and wishes. Once Stephen learned how to resolve these issues through discussions and a number of exercises we performed in therapy, he felt more confident and was picked on much less in school.

5. Mistaking nonassertiveness for being helpful. This is the child who grows up to become the rescuer who often actually fails to provide genuine help.

Joanne, sixteen years old, came to therapy because of poor scholastic performance and difficulty in concentrating. Joanne was the daughter of an alcoholic father and a mother who had engaged in enabling or rescuing behavior for many years. The mother had always been there for the father and never really condemned his drinking, even though it was so destructive of the family. Joanne learned the very same behaviors. She would wait at home, put the father to bed, take care of him, and call the father's boss with excuses for not being at work on Monday. Once she was taught to stop rescuing, to not give her father help he didn't need while sacrificing her own needs, her concentration at school and her general self-esteem improved a great deal.

6. Deficient skills are another reason children and adults behave unassertively. The child may simply not know how to act otherwise. He may not have learned the appropriate assertiveness skills because, for whatever reasons, he did not have an opportunity to observe how others handle similar situations.

Blaine, a young girl raised in several foster homes, never had the opportunity to observe a mother and father modeling or demonstrating, on an ongoing basis, assertive, problem-solving behavior regarding life's circumstances. I placed Blaine in group therapy, where, over the course of a year and a half, she was able to observe a number of other children learning to master a wide variety of situations. Finally, she was able to initiate the problem-solving skills successfully.

Recent psychological literature has identified a number of other tried and true ways to build up a child's confidence and self-esteem. The child who feels good about himself, who values and respects himself, and who believes he is valued by other significant people in his life, is far less likely to crave approval and to become overly dependent, needy, and desperate for approval, attention, and love.

The importance of promoting social skills cannot be overestimated. The child who grows up feeling comfortable with and valued by his peers is able to assert himself, respond effectively, and not crave approval as an adult. You must try to become aware of the extraordinary pressure your children experience every day to be like the other kids, in activities that range from learning to ski and play board games to how they dress, what curfew restrictions they have, and what TV shows they can watch. Children want to do what everyone else is doing. You as a parent are constantly faced with maintaining the very tricky balance between setting very clear limits for your children's behavior, particularly their physical and psychological safety, versus accepting slowly their obviously developmentally correct need to establish more and more autonomous lifestyles. This is one of the great dilemmas of parenthood. It must

be emphasized that developing social skills; learning how to nego-
tiate and solve problems, how to share, and how to identify all sorts
of verbal and nonverbal cues that occur from other children that
help them to understand what the other children are feeling and
thinking; dealing with aggressive feelings; and learning how to be
assertive can only be learned through time spent playing and
interacting with other children. Any opportunity to foster that
experience through play dates, day camps, after-school activities,
or the myriad of programs offered to children from ages three to
eighteen should be encouraged.

When you observe your children interacting with their peers, it
is important that you observe in such a way as to provide helpful,
constructive feedback to your children about the way they are
interacting. I trained Jan and her husband Todd how to give such
feedback to their thirteen-year-old daughter Sally. The type of
feedback I wanted them to give Sally was how to avoid being overly
dependent on the directions and authority of other children. Sally
would tend to admire girls who were a bit older than her, take her
cue from them, do what they told her to do, and sometimes be
manipulated and controlled into doing their dirty work. Sally's
parents observed this behavior in their home. I taught them how to
give constructive feedback to their daughter, how to point out that
when she gives up her self, she loses something very dear, that the
other children will take advantage of her, and that she has every
right to make her own decisions, to say no, and to stand up for her
needs and her rights. I worked with Jan and Todd to role play with
Sally, after they'd observed particular behaviors they believed were
inconsistent with being an autonomous or independent person,
behaviors that lead to approval craving and neediness. You can do
the same, first explaining to your child why such behaviors are not
useful, only lead to future trouble, and can only create a lack of
respect from those very admired peers that they are trying so hard
to impress. Then you can role play with your children, reenacting
those actual situations and training your children how to say no,
how to stand up for themselves, and so on.

Sally was very intimidated by her friends' threats not to be her
best friend if she didn't do what they instructed, such as relay

messages to boys and make faces and write silly notes to the teacher. The parents role played with Sally on how to say no to these friends, how to tell the other children to do their own dirty work and that she had better things to do. At first, Sally was very concerned about losing the other children's affection, but, as it turned out, when she took a stand, the other children tended to back off rather quickly, and Sally and her parents were very pleased with the results of the role play training.

We can't emphasize here enough the fact that children learn through rehearsal and corrective feedback.

Judicious self-disclosure by parents to their children about their own early life tendencies is often very helpful. Children don't believe that we as parents have the same fears, apprehensions, and anxieties that they do. Pointing out in a supportive and gentle way to children that we did have those feelings when we were younger and that their experiences are not unique but very similar to what we felt can be very helpful.

It is also useful when you are going through the role playing to have the child repeat out loud some of the distorted or irrational thoughts she might be having about what it might mean to lose this person's affection or approval. Some of the distorted thoughts we reviewed earlier in the book that applied to you can also be applied to your children. The children can make up their own age-relevant charts and tables with your help and can actually identify the fearful or irrational beliefs. "She won't be my friend anymore, and I couldn't stand that." "I must have her like me. No one else will like me."

Again, building self-esteem in children prevents approval craving. Children who value themselves and who feel good about themselves and what they do generally do not develop into approval cravers. It is the children who feel unworthy, unloved, and unlovable who crave approval and who will do just about anything to get it.

In a wonderful chapter by Judith McKay, "Building Self-Esteem in Children" found in *Self-Esteem: A Proven Program of Cognitive Techniques for Assessing and Improving and Maintaining Your Self-Esteem*, by Matthew McKay and Patrick Fanning (New Harbinger Publications, 1987), she points out a number of other skills parents can use to help enhance their children's self-esteem.

♦ *Listening.*

It is essential for the child's self-esteem that you find time to listen in an active, caring, and supportive way that communicates that what you are listening to is important and significant and deserves the attention of an adult. McKay suggests that you make sure you are ready to listen, that you won't be distracted by other activities that would ruin the moment. Give your child your entire attention; be an active listener who asks questions. Let the child know you are not tuning out but are very much with them at the moment. Encourage your child to verbalize her feelings and thoughts. Many children will do so automatically, but some will not, and they do need to be pulled out and encouraged.

♦ *Many parents feel they have to "fix" things.*

Many of us play Mr. or Mrs. Fix-it in our relationships with spouses or friends. They tell us a sad story and we feel compelled to jump in with a bandaid or a solution. Children often don't want that. They want to talk, to be heard, and they don't want to be interrupted with suggestions or advice. Perhaps most important, the child doesn't have the opportunity to work out his own problems and to find answers and solutions himself. He becomes more and more dependent on the parent. Even though he resents it, he will often capitulate to the advice because it's easy. Offering advice and being helpful is certainly good if the child solicits it, and is useful after a certain point has been reached. But the child first needs an opportunity to vent his feelings fully before you jump in and rescue him.

♦ *The language we use in our communication with our children is important.*

Feedback that enhances self-esteem has three components. First, use the language of description, not judgment. Don't judge the child in any way. Describe the behavior the child is engaging in. If the child acts up or has a temper tantrum, never say, "You are bad." Say, "That behavior is hurtful to your (sister, brother, and so on) and to me. When you behave like that, you create a lot of loud noises and a ruckus that interferes with my (studying, cooking, and so on) and your (sister's, brother's, naptime, playing, and so on)."

Then the parent needs to emphasize that the child is still lovable and not in any way bad, but that the behavior being described is not acceptable. How you react to the behavior is very important and communicates your disapproval or annoyance, your delight, joy, or pride to the child. Children need to grow up in an unambiguous, unconfused environment in which how they behave is communicated and fed back to them by the parent, with clarity about your feelings regarding your child's behavior, pro and con. Being open to sharing these feelings rather quickly and directly with the child—in a nonjudgmental way—shapes the child's self-esteem.

Finally, acknowledging her feelings means validating your child's experience, letting your child know that you understand the defeated feelings that she is having, the sadness, the feeling of loneliness and rejection, as well as the joy and pride she is taking in a job well done. Let your child know that her feelings are legitimate, valid, and that they are uniquely hers and that you are never judging those feelings.

In summary, description of the behavior, your reaction to the behavior, and your acknowledgment of the children's feelings are the three feedback elements that, according to McKay, affect self-esteem.

The following are active interventions you can train your child to use in order to prevent the development of approval-craving problems. I find that the most effective set of techniques in working with children is based on the work of Albert Ellis, founder of Rational Emotive Therapy. Rational emotive therapy is one of several cognitive behavioral interventions useful to teach children how to modify their unhealthy thoughts and beliefs. This intervention is generally based on the assumption that emotional problems in both children and adults result from faulty thinking about events, rather than from the events themselves. This system is best delineated by the "A, B, C" theory of emotional disturbance originally developed by Ellis. A is an activating event, B is beliefs about an event, and C is the emotional and behavioral consequence. D is disputing, which means challenging irrational beliefs by questioning assumptions about an event.

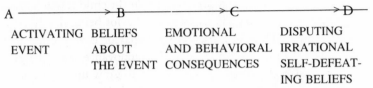

A ————————→ B ——————————→ C ————————————→ D

| ACTIVATING | BELIEFS | EMOTIONAL | DISPUTING |
| EVENT | ABOUT | AND BEHAVIORAL | IRRATIONAL |
| | THE EVENT | CONSEQUENCES | SELF-DEFEAT- |
| | | | ING BELIEFS |

Many people, particularly children, feel that A, activating events, actually create or cause consequences. Numerous studies and clinical evidence clearly demonstrate that it is the beliefs, B, about the event that intervene and truly determine the emotional and behavioral consequences that people feel. If beliefs are rational, make sense, are consistent with evidence, and are not distorted, they result in relatively moderate emotional reactions that allow people to react reasonably constructively and to reach their goals. On the other hand, irrational beliefs that are not based on logic or evidence and that are faulty in their construction, generally lead to very disturbed emotions such as rage, terror, and depression, thus interfering with achieving goals.

The basic core idea of this system is that emotional upset derives from three major irrational beliefs that lead to nonproductive feelings and attitudes such as awfulizing (catastrophizing), a sense of worthlessness, and "I can't stand it" thinking in children. The following are the three major irrational beliefs children experience.

1. "I must do well and win approval of all of my performances, or else I am a truly worthless person." This is a particularly important belief for approval cravers.
2. "Others must treat me considerately, in exactly the way I want them to treat me, and if they don't, they should be damned for their insensitivity to my very important needs."
3. "The conditions under which I live must be arranged so that I get nearly everything I want efficiently, comfortably, and immediately, and that I am subject to virtually nothing that I don't want."

Eileen, a fifteen-year-old girl, was constantly fighting with other children at school. The fights (A, the activating event) would nearly always start when one of the children teased her about her sophisticated way of dressing and making up. That would lead to Eileen becoming extremely upset, angry, and embarrassed—that is, C, the emotional consequence. Eileen erroneously assumed that if she was teased by these peers, this meant she would always be isolated at school, that the kids would continue to poke fun at her, and that initially they had believed she was unappealing and unattractive. These beliefs were B, the irrational thoughts.

I encouraged Eileen to dispute these beliefs and pointed out to her that first of all, she was demanding that the other children treat her precisely the way she felt they *should*, that they *should* understand and accept her clothing and her more sophisticated outlook, and that it was *terrible* and *absolutely dreadful* if they didn't. By asking Eileen a series of questions I also helped her dispute B, her irrational beliefs, and helped her put her problem in a more rational perspective and feel much less upset and angry. I asked her questions such as the following. "Just because some of the girls tease you, does it necessarily mean you won't have friends in school?" "Does it necessarily mean that they are right?" "Where is it written that the others must approve of the way you dress and look?" "Why can't there be differences of opinion?" "Is it really *terrible* and not merely a darn inconvenience that a few of the children act quite immaturely toward you? Why do they all have to be mature?" "You are in school with children, and children will often act like children." "What can you do to be a better friend in school or to not act quite so snobbish or supercilious so that these children will have less of a reason to tease you; that is, what actions can you take to reduce your vulnerability to the teasing, rather than do what you have been doing, which is to be open and vulnerable and passive about it?" "Do you not have the choice to find other friends with whom you can spend time?"

I encourage parents to use this "A,B,C,D," outline to help their children directly and vigorously identify and then dispute irrational beliefs based on the three overriding elements I detailed earlier to help them get through numerous problem situations. The goal here is to correct core irrational ideas.

A wonderful two-volume set of books by Ann Vernon, *Thinking, Feeling, and Behaving: An Emotional Education Curriculum for Children and Adolescents* (Research Press, Champagne, Illinois), describes a number of activities that both teachers and parents can use with children to help them actively undermine the irrational, distorted ideas that get them into trouble.

You can refer to the book for numerous activities, but the following are a few we have selected because of their special pertinence to approval craving. You can modify these exercises for younger children.

## *Who Counts?*

OBJECTIVE: To learn the importance of self-acceptance despite the risk of others' disapproval.

MATERIALS: Paper and pencils as needed.

PROCEDURE

1. Introduce the exercise by asking your child if he has ever done anything he felt good about but knew that his friends would laugh at or criticize. Ask for several examples.
2. Ask your child to listen to the following situations and be prepared to finish the scenarios by writing a response to each.

- Susan is smart and can get good grades without trying, but if she does raise her hand to answer all the time, finish early, or help others out, kids . . .
- Ted is really a good actor, but most of his friends are athletic. He's thinking of not trying out for the school play because . . .
- Debbie knows the difference between right and wrong, but she wants to fit in, too. When her friends encourage her to make fun of the teacher, she does it because . . .
- Don knows that cheating is wrong, but when the guys ask

him to let them look over his shoulder during a test, he does it because . . .

DISCUSSION

Content Question:

Were any of the situations familiar to you? Share examples.

Personalization Questions:

1. What have you done in situations of this nature?
2. How do you feel about yourself if you do something you know is wrong or something with which you aren't comfortable?
3. Do you think it is better to risk others' disapproval and feel good about yourself and your decisions or to do what your friends want?

## Approval and Consequences

OBJECTIVE: To recognize the advantages and disadvantages of doing something to gain social approval.

MATERIALS: Magazine pictures of people drinking beer, kissing, fighting, smoking, and so on, and paper and pencil.

PROCEDURE

1. Hold up the magazine pictures and ask your child to describe what she sees happening. Indicate that sometimes people do things because they want to, but other times because they want to be accepted by others. Ask your child to think of examples of things that could be done to get others' approval (taking drugs, making out, getting caught up in fad diets or clothing fads, and so on). List examples.
2. Discuss the difference between doing something because you feel it's right for you and doing something that doesn't feel right but that you do because the crowd is doing it and you want their approval. Discuss the concept of consequences of doing things for peer approval, using the following example.

Tony is a good student, but the kids he runs around with think doing homework and being smart means that you are a nerd. So Tony stops studying and gets bad grades so he'll fit in.

DISCUSSION

Content Questions:

1. What are some of the consequences that have to be considered when deciding whether or not to do something?
2. What happens if you go against the crowd and do what you think is right for you?

Personalization Questions:

1. When you are confronted with a conflict of this type, what process do you go through in deciding what to do?
2. If you go with the crowd but against what you think might be right for you, how do you feel?
3. Have you learned anything from this activity that you could apply to future conflict situations involving peer approval?

## Dependent and Independent Relationships

OBJECTIVE: To distinguish between dependent and independent behavior in relationships.

MATERIALS: Paper and pencil as needed.

PROCEDURE

1. Introduce this exercise by discussing the difference between dependence and independence. Dependence means that you rely on someone else for support or existence. Independence means that you rely on yourself for support. If you are independent, you are generally more confident of your abilities, more self-reliant, and more in control of yourself.
2. Write the words *dependent* and *independent* on a piece of paper. Engage in a brainstorming session with your child to identify

dependent and independent behaviors in relationships with others. List these under two separate columns on the paper. Examples of dependent versus independent behaviors might be sitting at home by the phone waiting for someone to call instead of finding something else to do, or constantly asking for reassurance about whether or not someone likes you as opposed to feeling confident about your self-worth.

3. Discuss whether or not anyone is totally dependent or independent, or whether this depends on the person or the circumstance. Draw a line on the paper to illustrate a continuum. Put the word *dependent* on one end and the word *independent* on the other. Have your child draw her own continuum on a piece of paper and mark it to identify whether she is more independent or dependent in the following areas: being in dating relationships, going to new places, and meeting new people.

4. Encourage your child to generate more areas in which she could express dependence or independence. Have her mark the continuum for each area she suggests.

DISCUSSION

Content Questions:

1. How can you distinguish dependent from independent behavior?

2. What did you learn about the various ways dependent behavior is shown?

Personalization Questions:

1. In general, do you think you are more dependent or independent in relationships? How do you feel about this?

2. Are there some areas that are more difficult for you than others?

3. Which type of behavior do you think is healthier for you in your relationships with others?

# *I Can't Live Without Him/Her*

OBJECTIVE: To differentiate between disappointment and devastation when a relationship terminates.

MATERIALS: Paper and pencil as needed.

PROCEDURE

1. To introduce the exercise, ask your child to think of a popular song, movie, or book in which the theme is "I can't live without you." Generally, this theme occurs when one partner in a relationship has broken up and the other partner feels devastated and doesn't think he or she can go on living.
2. Next, discuss reasons students think the person who has been left behind feels so devastated. Discuss the difference between feeling devastated and feeling very disappointed that the relationship ended.

DISCUSSION

Content Questions:

1. Do you think devastation or disappointment is the most common feeling when a relationship ends?
2. What could account for the difference between feeling devastated or disappointed? Which do you think is preferable?

Personalization Questions:

1. If you have ever felt devastated when a relationship ended, what did you do about your feelings?
2. What do you think you could do to prevent the feeling of devastation?

# SUMMARY

◆

As we completed this book I looked carefully through my case notes to get a better sense of exactly how the many people I have treated using this step program have fared on follow-up. How had they done after many months or a year or so of therapy using the principles we've been espousing in this book?

While we must caution you that this review was not a scientific one, there were certainly a number of significant and universal changes that had come about in the patients who had gone through this program. That is, most patients who had gone through the program, stuck with it, and made some of the changes they had desired, had reported some of the following changes.

♦ *The first and most important change these people described was what we would have predicted: a general and authentic reduction in the fear of disapproval, both from those who were close to them, as well as strangers, friends, and passing acquaintances. These former patients reported that this was the most profound change of all. It seemed to cut across sexes, age ranges, and socioeconomic groups. At the same time, these patients reported generally feeling much more assertive in their contacts and interactions with others.*

Remember Tina, whose story introduced this book? What can she look forward to? Now that she has read this book, her dreams, whether they take place in office settings or anywhere else, picture a more confident and competent Tina. Tina is now entirely comfortable allowing her husband, Ernie, to see her without makeup and with her hair messy. Tina has gained a little bit of weight and reports being only minimally concerned that her husband might not approve. If she does take off the weight, she will do it for herself, not because Ernie requires it. Tina is now more assertive with repairmen. Recently, she had her washing machine serviced and was quite assertive and confident in negotiating a fair price. She has learned to send out memos at work every time she develops a new creative idea to ensure that no one can steal her thunder. Tina is much more comfortable giving her public presentations, recognizing that she knows her material as well as anybody in the room. And while Tina still gets butterflies in her stomach before a public speaking situation, her level of anxiety is considerably reduced. Tina has demanded that Ernie and she go for couples therapy because she can no longer tolerate his belligerent, humiliating tone in public or in private. The therapist has agreed with Tina on a number of her demands in the relationship and she is working hard with Ernie to make sure he understands her needs and is responsive to them. She also has become much more clear about what she wants from Ernie romantically and she is not there merely to service him.

Tina's is an apocryphal story; it reflects many of the universal changes that occur in many of the people who go through this step program.

♦ *The second relatively universal change we've seen in people who've gone through the program is that they've generally achieved happier relationships. They talk less of bailing out of their relationships and more of working collaboratively and cooperatively with their partner to make the relationship a better one. They no longer feel recriminations from their partners when they assert themselves. They no longer are as dependent on their partners for help in making decisions, and they report generally feeling much more pride in the relationship and in themselves for being decisive and independent. A number of these patients now report they've been able to take vacations without their spouses or partners for the first time in their lives. This is truly a major step for these people who until going through this program were terrified that it would garner their spouse's or partner's disapproval. These folks also report much fewer fights, better sex, more cooperation in raising children, more comfort in going out with other couples, and having an all-around better social life. Also, they report in their relationships that when they engage in sports and other athletics with each other, there is friendly competition with a real sense that each is going to help the other learn the skills of the sport better, rather than fearing they will be criticized if they make a mistake.*

♦ *The third universal change we have observed in those who have undergone the approval-addiction step program could be labeled "freedom from unwanted bad habits, phobias, and chronic worrying." This is kind of a catch-all category. What we mean by that is that most of those who have gone through the program report that many of the maladaptive habits, such as nail biting, various tics (funny body or facial expressions), fears (of elevators, small animals, heights, or going out of the home), and chronic worrying (in which a person just cannot get particular themes out of her mind, rehearsing and reviewing them incessantly, anticipating problems that will occur in the future), seem to improve a great deal when approval-addiction has been successfully tackled. There are several explanations for this. It is particularly important to note that many of these changes occurred without actually addressing the bad habits, fears, worrying, and tics directly. It's almost as if this were a bonus of the treatment. As people become more assertive, confident, and stop worrying as much about others liking them and are less concerned about their image, their confidence level improves and they generate a stronger and stronger sense of control over their own lives.*

This sense of control, of self-destiny, frequently provides them with the wherewithal to overcome these habits, phobias, and obsessive worrying problems. They feel that they are more masters of their own destiny and not dependent on others to direct and guide them. As they change that perception of themselves in relation to others, many of these habits and phobias that were born out of feelings of inadequacy and victimization give way, even if they are not addressed directly.

♦ *A fourth universal area that seems to change for approval-addicted people who undergo the program is that they report a greater sense of altruism, a greater desire to help others. This is accompanied by appearing and feeling much less self-absorbed. They are more trusting of others, more willing to defend and support others. They insulate themselves less and less and become more open and accessible emotionally. They are more willing to share their emotions honestly with others, rather than hiding behind a facade of defensiveness, humor, or anger. These people frequently report an increase in their willingness to do volunteer work, an improvement in their relationships with older parents, and greater willingness to be available to help friends. But it is important to note that this altruism is more healthy. They are not available as victims, as people to be exploited or taken advantage of, but as confident, empowered, self-aware beings. In the past, out of a genuine fear of being exploited, they would shy away from situations in which they might be called upon to give of their expertise, to volunteer time, or to be emotionally available to others. After the program, that fear seems to have been dissolved and they are more capable of being available in a genuine way to others.*

I'm reminded of Phyllis, who, after thirty or thirty-five sessions of therapy in our approval-craving program, reported to me that she thought much less about her own problems and issues and spent a great deal more time being concerned with world issues. She had become involved in peace foundations she had always wanted to assist but had never before had the confidence and sense of worthiness to join.

♦ *A fifth major change in post-program patients is reports of better physical health. This is consistent with numerous studies coming from laboratories that suggest that the immune system as well as other important physiological systems of the body are sensitive to stress. As stress decreases or as a person learns more effective coping strategies to deal with stress, their immune system improves, their brain chemistry may change, blood pressure comes under control, dermatological problems recede (including some types of hair loss), sexual prowess improves, colitis and other stomach disorders disappear, and asthma conditions improve. There's even some evidence that rheumatoid arthritis is directly related to stress. The point is that as approval craving recedes, general health can improve as well—a most welcome change.*

The issue of growing comfortable, confident, secure, and assertive in our interpersonal relationships has never been more important than it is now. Because we live in an era of AIDS, many people will remain in relationships that may not be satisfying, for fear of moving out into the single world and tackling the issue of safe sex. In order to hold onto these partners, they become even more compliant and fearful of rejection. The recession has kept some in relationships out of fear of financial deprivation. In the workplace, many are tolerating uncomfortable and unfair conditions in docile, compliant manners out of the fear that they may not be able to find another job. It is for these people in particular that an increase in assertiveness and comfort in making demands is necessary, even life-saving. A general disillusionment with the progress of the Women's Movement impinges on the subject of approval craving as well. While numerous gains have been made for equality between the sexes, economic parity is still a distant dream. Many crucial rights, such as the right to an abortion, are imperiled, and recently highly publicized rape and sexual harassment cases indicate that in many quarters women are still considered second-class citizens. That societal view is easily internalized by women, who must continually work on fighting an inferior image and maintaining an inner sense of independence.

A random sample of conversations overheard at parties, restaurants, bus stops, and offices reveals continuing references to "Why doesn't he like me more?," "Why doesn't he like me?," "I would do anything to get him," and so on. This issue of approval craving is still high on the American agenda. Any Twelve Step program (AA,

GA, NA, or OA) meeting is taken up with horror stories of enablers, particularly women, sticking to their significant other, not confronting their negative behavior—even reinforcing it by staying in the relationship and continuing to love, adore, worship, and attend to the addict's needs—while they continue to be abused and exploited. Approval craving is endemic among people who have addiction problems and their families.

We have tried in this book to provide you with an action plan to first identify this problem, and, second, to overcome it. Whereas other books have been written on assertiveness and relationships, we believe that this book provides a practical recipe for identifying the aspects of approval craving and then helping you work on resolving this problem. The numerous clients we have discussed in this book are the heroes here, because they have labored, both on their own and in therapy, to overcome their terror of rejection. The truth is, none of us ever wants to be rejected, and all of us, as social creatures, naturally work toward affiliation and acceptance by others, but many of us are obsessed with acceptance and terrified by rejection. Many of the clients we discussed here have successfully overcome these problems and are now living free and liberated lives. To these people we dedicate this book. They are the pioneers.